CONFRONTING TODAY'S WORLD

A Fundamentalist Looks at Social Issues

CONFRONTING TODAY'S WORLD

A Fundamentalist Looks at Social Issues

L. DUANE BROWN

Regular Baptist Press
1300 North Meacham Road
Post Office Box 95500
Schaumburg, Illinois 60195

Library of Congress Cataloging-in-Publication Data

Brown, L. Duane, 1933–
    Confronting today's world.

    Includes bibliographies.
    1. Fundamentalism. 2. Evangelicalism. 3. Church and
social problems. I. Title.
BT82.2.B76 1986   261.8   85-28294
ISBN 0-87227-108-0

CONFRONTING TODAY'S WORLD:
A FUNDAMENTALIST LOOKS AT SOCIAL ISSUES

Dedication

I dedicate this book to the people of Southwest Calvary Baptist Church, Houston, Texas. My happy, fruitful years in the busiest, noisiest city in America will always be treasured.

Appreciation

This book could not have been completed without sacrificial help. I want to thank my wife for her patience and for her expert help in the preparation of the book. A special salute to Joanne Audas who typed the manuscript.

Contents

Introduction   9

I. Research from Scripture
2 Timothy 2:15

1 Scriptures for the Support of Believers   19
2 Scriptures for the Support of Unbelievers   21
3 'Who Is My Neighbor?'   25

II. Repudiation of False Views
Colossians 2:8

4 Socialism and the Social Gospel   31
5 The Cultural Mandate   41
6 Reformed Theology   45
7 New Evangelicalism   51

III. Responsibility of the Church
1 Timothy 3:15

8 The Intention of the Church   63
9 The Individuals of the Church   73

IV. Review of Social Issues
Galatians 6:10

10 Abortion: The Murder of Society   81
11 Alcoholism: The Curse of Society   87
12 Crime: The Violence in Society   101
13 Divorce and Remarriage: The Breakdown of
      Society   105
14 Drugs: The Insanity of Society   111

15   Euthanasia: The Rejected of Society   117
16   Femininity vs. Feminism: The Struggle in
        Society   121
17   Gambling: The Weakness in Society   125
18   Genetic Engineering: The Fear of Society   129
19   Homosexuality: The Menace to Society   135
20   Hunger and Poverty: The Needy of Society   139
21   Sexual Abuse: The Victims of Society   145
22   Suicide: The Heartache of Society   157
23   War and Self-Defense: The Protection of
        Society   161

V. Restatement of Biblical Position
2 Peter 3:13, 14

Conclusion   169
Bibliography   175

Introduction

The world is a mess! The threat of nuclear destruction; the sight of bloated, starving children; and the horrible fact of the annual murder of over one million unborn babies in the United States are but a few of the social wounds of this unjust generation. The question facing Bible believers who stand on the Word of God as our chart and course of life is, What shall we do about these issues? Should the church of Jesus Christ seek to change the world? Does compassion justify and motivate the church to invest the Lord's money and servants into these just causes? How and how much should those who are called fundamentalists seek to answer the cries of the victims of social injustice?

The answers to these questions must come from the Bible. Do the Scriptures direct us to reform the world and to heal the hurt of people oppressed by disease, tyranny, prejudice and selfishness? Besides drawing on the Scriptures themselves, I will give the conclusions of many religious leaders as well as my own conclusions, which have come from more than twenty-five years of experience, not only as a pastor, but also as state representative of Regular Baptist state associations. I have served as president of the American Council of Christian Churches, which has also served to broaden my perspective on these issues.

Make no mistake about it, fundamentalists are under fire. We are accused of the lack of compassion, of copping out on the real world and of failing to obey our Lord. The Wheaton Declaration of 1966 composed by sincere and troubled evangelicals stated:

> We have sinned grievously. We are guilty of an unscriptural isolation from the world that too often keeps us from honestly facing and coping with its concerns. We have failed to apply scriptural principles to such problems as racism, war, population explosion, poverty, family disintegration, social revolution and communism.

Now these critics are not only repenting, but in fact criticizing those of us who have not joined with them in this change of heart and philosophy. The distinguished journalist, Sherwood Eliot Wirt, related his newfound experience with these words:

> Churches whose orientation is toward the Bible are learning that a serious study of the social context of God's revelation is a rich mine of spiritual teaching. They are becoming acquainted with the world to which they are called to carry the Gospel.[1]

So there it is. We nonactivists in social issues are either ignorant or disobedient!

Perhaps the most significant criticism of the fundamentalist position of noninvolvement came in 1947 when a series of articles appeared in the now defunct publication *Religious Digest*, and later printed in the book, *The Uneasy Conscience of Modern Fundamentalism*, where the highly recognized scholar, Carl F. H. Henry, unloaded his bomb on fundamentalists with this blast:

> There is a growing awareness in Fundamentalism circles that, despite the orthodoxy insistence upon revelation and redemption, evangelical Christianity has become increasingly inarticulate about the social reference of the Gospel. . . . Fundamentalism is wondering just how it is that a world changing message narrowed its scope to the changing of isolated individuals. . . . The failure of the evangelical movement to react favorably on any widespread front to campaign against social evils has led, finally, to a suspicion on the part of non-evangelicals that there is something in the very nature of Fundamentalism which makes a world ethical view impossible.[2]

Dr. Henry, while still identifying himself as a fundamentalist (which he later discarded), wants to throw out the baby with the bath water. He claimed fundamentalism did not just have a flaw, but it was ethically bankrupt.

But these men seem mild when compared to a more recent critic, Richard Quebedeaux, in his book *The Young Evangelicals*. He analyzed the traditionalist view of fundamentalism with this denunciation:

> In their zeal to defend the faith against criticism, Fundamentalists and Evangelicals have given too many pat answers to profound questions. And by capitalizing on numerical strength, they have overlooked something very important about the Gospel. For if Liberals have reduced Christian faith to humanism, holders of the Orthodox position have been guilty of neglecting the social dimension of the Gospel entirely—seeking the salvation of souls but allowing bodies to go to hell. Fundamentalists and perhaps most Evangelicals have dismissed the biblical principle that faith without works is dead—that grace without discipleship is "cheap grace." They have too often ignored the fact that a new relationship with God in Jesus Christ calls for a new relationship with men and women. Orthodoxy has forgotten that Christian commitment, at its deepest level, is a narrow way not easily found—a path over which the disciple of Christ must always take up his cross. And history shows us that the way of the cross is never popular. In twentieth-century America, such action may result in persecution by the government and a pharisaic church when a Christian takes the side of the oppressed and in so doing prophetically challenges structured social evils (Matthew 5:11, 12).[3]

Robert Webber, professor at Wheaton College, wrote a book on how the believer should deal with the issue of Christianity's relation to society. The book, which was financed through a grant by the alumni of the college, is entitled *The Secular Saint*. The author summarized the evangelical choices into three categories. The first is the separatist view which was drawn from the Western world. It can be summarized with these characteristics: The way of living is paramount for the Christian; this life must be lived apart from the world and is best lived in communities which are equated with the kingdom of God.

The second type (which would characterize most fundamentalists) is called the Identification Model. It holds, with considerable variety, that God works through both the church and the state and the Christian has obligations to both, causing tension and making it difficult to maintain a balance.

The third view (which Webber as a new evangelical would espouse) supports the Transformational Model which attempts to change society. It holds that Christ's redemption reaches into culture, and the church is the means of restoring the world and man to the original intent of God by its example and influence.

Dr. Webber believes the church's neglect of society's problems in the first half of the twentieth century was due to the rise of dispensationalism, which emphasized the end times, thus giving a pessimistic mood. As a result evangelism lost its social emphasis and sought to rescue souls. However, since 1960 there has been a renewed sense of the social implication of the gospel. This is caused, Webber thinks, by a changing cultural climate, a demise of the theological liberal social outreach and the rise of many younger evangelicals who are social activists. He feels the Chicago Declaration by the evangelicals who met in 1973 has set the pace and mood for this change. This declaration calls for an active battle against social evils in North America.[4]

Another popular publication is *The Mustard Seed Conspiracy* by Tom Sine. His thesis is that Christians are like mustard seeds in society and our duty is to think positively about the changing world. He says, "So welcome to the conspiracy of the insignificant, invisible, and incomprehensible! God wants to use your small contribution to join others in transforming his world today and tomorrow."[5]

Other publications have appeared which display a passion for arousing the evangelical church to social action. Some of the publications are: *Decision, Christianity Today, The Other Side, Evangelical Newsletter, Eternity, World Evangelization* and *Post American*. Organizations which promote social action are the National and World Councils of Churches, the National Association of Evangelicals, and Evangelicals for Social Action. Colleges and seminaries which major in this philosophy include Bethel Seminary, Fuller Seminary, Wheaton College, Gordon-Conwell Seminary and College, Conservative Baptist Seminary and the Southern Baptist schools. (George Dollar in his book *A History of Fundamentalism in America* attempts to list and classify these organizations.[6]) Some of the nationally known evangelicals who have spoken out for social action are Billy Graham, Carl Henry, Vernon Grounds, Paul Rees, Harold John Ockenga,

Ronald Sider and Harold Lindsell. A well-known, self-named fundamentalist who advocates social action is Jerry Falwell. (His views will be evaluated in a later chapter.)

The traditional fundamentalist view was stated by I. M. Haldeman, the long-time pastor of First Baptist Church, New York City, now with Christ. He said:

> The Church is not here to decorate the world and sing siren songs of hope, cry peace when there is no peace, but to save men out of the world. There are three ways in which the church is to do this:
>
> First, by preaching the Gospel.
>
> Second, by invoking and surrendering to the operative power of the Holy Ghost.
>
> Third, by individual rescue work, the impingement of personal life upon personal life.[7]

Support for the fundamentalist viewpoint is contained in a pamphlet written by missionary-physician Donn W. Ketcham and published by the Association of Baptists for World Evangelism entitled, *The World Hurts!* Dr. Ketcham wrestles with his own convictions and conscience on the Biblical justification for medical missions. His conclusion is to repudiate the social gospel and to warn against the call of the new evangelicals for a social mandate. He makes a distinction between the church's responsibility, which is limited to evangelism, and the individual Christian who may participate in both spiritual and social ministries.[8] This unique dichotomy will be explored and evaluated in a later chapter.

Another helpful source is a series of studies in the *Bibliotheca Sacra* published by Dallas Theological Seminary. The writer, Charles C. Ryrie, brings an inductive study on the history and theology of Christian social activitists. He also traces the teachings of the Old and New Testaments on this subject.

The sources for social action philosophy are multiple indeed. Sider, Mott, Webber, Wagner, Price, Hughes, Smedes, Escobar, Doesak, Wallis, Perkins, Mouw are just a few of the recent authors to cry out for changes in the church's theology and priorities.

I recently visited Gordon-Conwell Seminary to research their library on this subject. Their faculty is often noted for this new-evangelical perspective. I interviewed the Professor of Social Ethics,

Stephen Charles Mott, who graciously advised me on the trends and latest books written on this area. His view can be fairly well summed up this way: one of the key tasks of the church is to gain social justice while still preaching the gospel. Evangelism and social action go together; they are on a parity. His book, *Social Ethics*, is a major contribution to the subject of social action.

In our fellowship of Regular Baptists, which is no doubt the "right wing" of all national church organizations, the facts show that social concern is a rather low priority. True, we have several wonderful children's agencies, at least one home for senior citizens, plus Shepherds Baptist Ministries for the mentally retarded; and, yes, we have a number of missionary hospitals and dispensaries on several foreign fields. But these are small investments.

William Brock said in his message at the annual conference of the General Association of Regular Baptist Churches in June 1983, that our social agencies are sadly neglected. In 1982 only about 1.2 percent to 1.5 percent of the churches' giving went to the approved social agencies. He feels this area of ministry deserves greater interest and investment.

Another viewpoint is presented by David Marshall, General Director of Evangelical Baptist Missions. He believes that the trends in social ministries by our mission agencies are highly questionable in the light of Scripture. He further believes these social projects drain off funds which ought to go to missionaries.[9] On the other side of the issue, W. Wilbert Welch, Chancellor of Grand Rapids Baptist College and Seminary, concludes that fundamentalists cannot remain noninvolved with current social evils (with certain guidelines and safeguards.)[10]

We are indebted to William Tracy Commons who researched the views of various Regular Baptist leaders for Informissions in 1976. His paper is a compilation of responses of forty-two pastors, professors, agency administrators and missionaries. Most agreed that social concern is a valid dimension for missions but with certain guidelines. It must be a secondary emphasis and a limited means of reaching the unsaved.[11]

Before those of us who call ourselves fundamentalists begin to agonize over what little we do for social needs, we need to review God's Word for direction. It has the power "for reproof, for correction, for instruction in righteousness" (2 Tim. 3:16).

Notes:

1. Sherwood Eliot Wirt, *The Social Conscience of the Evangelical* (New York: Harper & Row, 1968), p. 9.

2. Carl F. H. Henry, *The Uneasy Conscience of Modern Fundamentalism* (Grand Rapids: Wm. B. Eerdmans, 1947), pp. 23, 26.

3. Richard Quebedeaux, *The Young Evangelicals* (New York: Harper & Row, 1974), pp. 16, 17.

4. Robert E. Webber, *The Secular Saint* (Grand Rapids: Zondervan Publishing House, 1981) pp. 75–165.

5. Tom Sine, *The Mustard Seed Conspiracy* (Waco, TX: Word Books, 1981), p. 20.

6. George W. Dollar, *A History of Fundamentalism in America* (Greenville, SC: Bob Jones University Press, 1973), pp. 283–289.

7. I. M. Haldeman, "The Mission of the Church in the World," *The Biblical Evangelist* (September 3, 1982), 8.

8. Donn W. Ketcham, *The World Hurts!* (Cherry Hill, NJ: Association of Baptists for World Evangelism, 1981), pp. 35–40.

9. David Marshall, "Social Ministries—Are They Valid?" (Kokomo, IN: Evangelical Baptist Missions, n.d.).

10. W. Wilbert Welch, "The Church and Its Social Ministry," *Messenger* (June 1973), 2.

11. William Tracy Commons, "What Are We Doing in Social Concern?" Informissions, 1976.

I

Research from Scripture

"Study to shew thyself approved unto God, a work-man that needeth not to be ashamed, rightly dividing the word of truth" (2 Timothy 2:15).

1

Scriptures for the Support of Believers

When the serious Bible student searches out passages which would teach or even imply that believers should change society, he does not find very much. However, there are clear commands that Christians should care for *other believers* in their needs.

Hereby perceive we the love of God, because he laid down his life for us: and we ought to lay down our lives for the brethren.

But whoso hath this world's good, and seeth his brother have need, and shutteth up his bowels of compassion from him, how dwelleth the love of God in him?

My little children, let us not love in word, neither in tongue; but in deed and in truth (1 John 3:16–18).

Pure religion and undefiled before God and the Father is this, To visit the fatherless and widows in their affliction, and to keep himself unspotted from the world (James 1:27).

For to their power, I bear record, yea, and beyond their power they were willing of themselves;

Praying us with much intreaty that we would receive the gift, and take upon us the fellowship of the ministering to the saints.

Wherefore shew ye to them, and before the churches, the proof of your love, and of our boasting on your behalf (2 Cor. 8:3, 4, 24).

For as touching the ministering to the saints, it is superfluous for me to write to you:
For the administration of this service not only supplieth the want of the saints, but is abundant also by many thanksgivings unto God;
Whiles by the experiment of this ministration they glorify God for your professed subjection unto the gospel of Christ, and for your liberal distribution unto them, and unto all men (2 Cor. 9:1, 12, 13).

As we have therefore opportunity, let us do good unto all men, especially unto them who are of the household of faith (Gal. 6:10).

But if any provide not for his own, and specially for those of his own house, he hath denied the faith, and is worse than an infidel.
Let not a widow be taken into the number under threescore years old, having been the wife of one man,
Well reported of for good works; if she have brought up children, if she have lodged strangers, if she have washed the saints' feet, if she have relieved the afflicted, if she have diligently followed every good work.
If any man or woman that believeth have widows, let them relieve them, and let not the church be charged; that it may relieve them that are widows indeed (1 Tim. 5:8, 9, 10, 16).

Distributing to the necessity of saints; given to hospitality (Rom. 12:13).

These passages clearly command believers to share their material goods with needy Christians. Some of these apply to the local church as an organization and some apply to believers as individuals.

2

Scriptures
for the Support
of Unbelievers

Having looked at the passages of Scripture which teach that believers should care for other believers in need, let us now look at those passages which imply that Christians have a duty toward the social needs of the unsaved.

> As we have therefore opportunity, let us do good unto all men, especially unto them who are of the household of faith (Gal. 6:10).

> Bless them which persecute you: bless, and curse not.
> Therefore if thine enemy hunger, feed him; if he thirst, give him drink: for in so doing thou shalt heap coals of fire on his head.
> Be not overcome of evil, but overcome evil with good (Rom. 12:14, 20, 21).

> But I say to you, do not resist him who is evil; but whoever slaps you on your right cheek, turn to him the other also.
> And if any one wants to sue you, and take your shirt, let him have your coat also.
> And whoever shall force you to go one mile, go with him two.
> Give to him who asks of you, and do not turn away from him who wants to borrow from you.

You have heard that it was said, "You shall love your neighbor, and hate your enemy."

But I say to you, love your enemies, and pray for those who persecute you (Matt. 5:39–44, NASB).

. . . Thou shalt love the Lord thy God . . . and thy neighbor as thyself (Luke 10:27).

But a certain Samaritan, as he journeyed, came where he was: and when he saw him, he had compassion on him,

And went to him, and bound up his wounds, pouring in oil and wine, and set him on his own beast, and brought him to an inn, and took care of him.

And on the morrow when he departed, he took out two pence, and gave them to the host, and said unto him, Take care of him; and whatsoever thou spendest more, when I come again, I will repay thee (Luke 10:33–35).

And Jesus went about all the cities and villages, teaching in their synagogues, and preaching the gospel of the kingdom, and healing every sickness and every disease among the people.

But when he saw the multitudes, he was moved with compassion on them, because they fainted, and were scattered abroad, as sheep having no shepherd.

Then saith he unto his disciples, The harvest truly is plenteous, but the labourers are few;

Pray ye therefore the Lord of the harvest, that he will send forth labourers into his harvest (Matt. 9:35–38).

Being enriched in every thing to all bountifulness, which causeth through us thanksgiving to God (2 Cor. 9:11).

It is a fair conclusion that *none* of these passages gives a clear command that believers have a duty to provide for the needy of the world, nor to change the political structure of society, nor to challenge the inequities, prejudices and evils which plague mankind. Believers surely are to be compassionate and sensitive to others' needs, and they are to relieve suffering and sorrow. Furthermore, Christians are to love their neighbors, and love motivates to action;

so a genuine burden ought to characterize believers as a general quality of life (Rom. 13:8–10).

Also, the believer has a definite obligation to support his government in its administration of good, even if it is limited and often misguided (Rom. 13:1–8). He is to honor the king (1 Pet. 3:17). He is to be loyal to civil authorities and obey them (Titus 3:1). In society he is to be known by his example of faithfulness and piety (Titus 2:1–10). Employees should be honest and hard working (Eph. 6:5–8), and masters themselves should be just and honest (6:9).

Jesus did not challenge the evils of His own Jewish society but generally avoided them. He declined to correct the injustice of a selfish brother who refused to divide the family inheritance with this statement, "Man, who made me a judge or divider over you?" (Luke 12:14).

Jesus disappointed His disciples by not delivering Israel from the Roman oppression (Luke 24:21). Even at His ascension Jesus rejected the pressure from His disciples to "restore again the kingdom to Israel" (Acts 1:6). He refused the multitude's desire to make Him king (John 6:15).

Obviously the apostolic agenda did not include correcting social injustice. The apostles did not attack the most brutal social evil of their day: slavery. While not condoning slavery, the apostolic doctrine encouraged slaves to be faithful laborers "as to the Lord" (Eph. 6:7). They were to be "obedient unto their own masters, and to please them well in all things, not answering again" (Titus 2:9). One scholar noted, "Paul has no word of criticism for the institution [slavery] as such. In this sense, he was unconcerned about 'social ethics'—the impact of the gospel on social structures."[1]

A very helpful insight into the apostle Paul's philosophy and methodology is seen in his two years of missionary labors in Ephesus. This city was one of the largest of its day and one of the most corrupt, morally and spiritually. Yet when the riot broke out over the loss in influence and income brought on by the lack in sales of the idols of Diana, the city magistrate defended the missionaries with, "For ye have brought hither these men, which are neither robbers of churches, nor yet blasphemers of your goddess" (Acts 19:37). Paul's success was in soul-winning and preaching Christ (Acts 20:20, 21), not in changing the social or political evils of Ephesus. He was not a politician, but an evangelist!

Since Christians are to love their neighbors, this would necessitate kindly responses and assistance wherever they can. As individual citizens and neighbors, Christians in their benevolence are far different from the organized ministry of the church, either local or collective. A future chapter will examine the New Testament directions for the church. Perhaps the pointed statement of John Witmer sums up the teaching of Scripture:

> Absolutely no evidence exists that the apostolic church projected even one solution for the most pressing world problems of its day. . . . The import of the Bible evidence is that whatever was accomplished was not realized through a social program or a social impact, but rather by the power of God the Holy Spirit as the message of the Gospel was preached to individuals.[2]

Notes:

1. Charles C. Ryrie, "Perspectives on Social Ethics, Part IV," *Bibliotheca Sacra* (October—December 1977), 325, citing George E. Ladd, *A Theology of the New Testament*, p. 529.

2. John A. Witmer, "Christian Social Responsibility," *Bibliotheca Sacra* (July—September 1953), 217.

3

'Who Is
My Neighbor?'

This question was put to Jesus by a "certain lawyer" who was attempting to justify himself (Luke 10:29). Jesus had turned the tables on the man's trick question. He had hoped to trap Jesus so that he could accuse Him of heresy. The issue was fulfilling the Mosaic Law. What does the responsibility of loving your neighbor involve?

Jesus explained in the parable of the Good Samaritan that loving one's neighbor involves showing mercy on the helpless and needy. What is the application of this?

Stephen Mott identifies the neighbor as follows: "Your neighbors include the 'neighbor' who would seem to be excluded by definition: the enemy, the opposing ethnic, religious, or economic group. It is any person in need whom one encounters."[1]

Dr. Mott continues his argument that the object of love and hence action by believers should extend to all the human race, to all the world in its problems. He states, "People are candidates for our love because they are our fellow *human beings*. . . . Dignity was bestowed upon humanity in the fact of the Incarnation."[2]

He expands on this thesis that the believer's obligation extends to all men by quoting the existentialist Kierkegaard, "Your neighbor is every man. . . ."[3] He concludes that all men are equal and worthy of the believer's social concern.

But is this logic the correct interpretation of Scripture? The quotation, "Love thy neighbour as thyself" is based upon Leviticus 19:18. This instruction was given directly to Israel for their responsibility to care for others. Who were they to provide for and to protect? All of the nations or the Gentiles? No. Their obligation was fivefold: orphans and widows (Exod. 22:21–24), the poor (Exod. 23:6), the Levites (Deut. 26:12) and the "stranger that is within thy gates" (Deut. 5:14; 10:19). There were limits on who these neighbors were.

Richard D. Patterson describes Israel's social obligation with this observation:

> Throughout the Old Testament, then, the cause of the widow, the orphan, and the poor is particularly enjoined upon Israel as befitting a redeemed people who are entrusted with the character and standards of their Redeemer. Even in the last book, the theme is utilized in pointing to the coming ministry of the forerunner of Messiah and of Messiah Himself and of the righteousness that would then be inaugurated (Mal. 3:1–6).[4]

To probe deeper the divine mandate for social responsibility taught in the Old Testament, the excellent article by Charles Ryrie, "Old Testament Perspectives on Social Ethics," should be examined. Dr. Ryrie raises the question of limiting "neighbor" with this, ". . . Did God expect Israel to treat the poor of all nations as she was expected to treat her own poor?"[5]

Dr. Ryrie points out that many of the social problems of Israel (as well as those of other nations) came from their wicked, idolatrous religions. Foreigners, or strangers who settled in Israel, were afforded some provision (Deut. 26:12, 13). But interest could be taken from them (Deut. 23:20) but not from an Israelite.[6] Ryrie further observes:

> The theocratic laws govern only those who belong to the theocracy. It is vain to search in the Bible for laws that govern those outside the theocracy. Only as strangers become settlers do they come under the requirements and protection of the laws of the theocracy.[7]

The conclusion of Dr. Ryrie is significant as he rejects the commonly accepted idea that the Old Testament teaches a dynamic, aggressive social action for believers toward the world. He states the following:

The Old Testament perspective on social ethics focuses on concern for the oppressed and on righteous living within the group. It does not command the establishment of justice in the world, nor the care of all the oppressed in the world. It gives no example for involvement in the rough-and-tumble of political life. It *does* show God's love for justice and holiness in personal living as well as in the community life of the theocracy. It shows God's abiding hatred of sin. The social ethics of the Old Testament are much more "isolationist" than those of the New Testament.[8]

To make Luke 10:25–37, the parable of the Good Samaritan, teach that social causes are priority does not hold up. The purpose of Jesus was to reveal to the deceitful lawyer that he was quoting the Law but not obeying it. Since the Jewish scribe (the lawyer) would not recognize a Samaritan as *his* neighbor (the common view of the Jews in Jesus' day), he surely could not claim to fulfill the Law's second precept, "Love thy neighbor as thyself." Rather, he needed to see his sinfulness and lack of fulfilling the Law. After all, this is the purpose of the Law, namely, to reveal sin (Rom. 3:20). Jesus was not teaching social obligations; He was bringing a proud Jew to the recognition of his hypocrisy and sin. He needed to *believe* in the God of the Law before he could *serve* Him through the Law.

Notes:

1. Stephen Charles Mott, *Biblical Ethics and Social Change* (New York: Oxford University Press, 1982), p. 45.
2. Ibid., p. 46.
3. Ibid., p. 50.
4. Richard D. Patterson, "The Widow, the Orphan, and the Poor in the Old Testament and the Extra-Biblical Literature," *Bibliotheca Sacra* (July—September 1973), 232.
5. Charles C. Ryrie, "Perspectives on Social Ethics, Part II," *Bibliotheca Sacra* (April—June 1977), 116.
6. Ibid., p. 119.
7. Ibid., p. 120.
8. Ibid., p. 122.

II

Repudiation
of False
Views

"Beware lest any man spoil you through philosophy and vain deceit, after the tradition of men, after the rudiments of the world, and not after Christ" (Colossians 2:8).

4

Socialism
and the
Social Gospel

Socialism is more than a method of economics. It reveals a philosophy of life. It is atheistic, humanistic and materialistic. Its effect on society is seen by a number of various, yet similar, ideologies such as communism, fascism, social democracy, Islamic socialism, Third-World socialism and Fabian socialism. Its influence on the world's population is staggering. As of 1978 the advance of socialistic rule claimed fifty-three of the world's sovereign states, controlling 39 percent of the world's territory and 42 percent of its population.[1]

Socialism may well be the means by which the nations will be bound together in the end of this age. The Bible teaches that Antichrist will become a world tyrant, even to the point of receiving adulation and worship (Rev. 13). One of the branches of socialism is communism. History records its phenomenal influence in enslaving people. It has capitalized on political unrest, ignorance, poverty and hunger.

But the real danger of socialism, and communism in particular, is not its political and social impact, but its spiritual ramifications. Karl Marx, the founder of communism as a political system, may well have been motivated by power from Satan. Richard Wurmbrand sets forth the proposition that Marx was a satanist. He states:

> We begin to understand what has happened to young

31

Marx. He had had Christian convictions but had not led a consistent life. . . . Then he might have fallen in with the tenets of the highly secret Satanist Church and received the rites of initiation. Satan, whom his worshippers see in their hallucinatory orgies, speaks through them. Thus, Marx is only Satan's mouthpiece when he utters the words, "I wish to avenge myself against the one who rules above."[2]

Wurmbrand examines the young adult years of Marx. The fiery crusader abandoned Christianity. Before he embraced his atheistic socialism, he wrote several poems which expressed his search for Satan. Wurmbrand says:

Marx adopted Satan after an inner fight. The poems were ended in a period of severe illness, the result of this tempest within his heart. He writes at that time about his "vexation of having to make an idol of a view he detests. He feels sick."[3]

Whether or not Marx was a true satanist, he was surely used by Satan to give the philosophical basis for godless communism. The fact that nearly one-half of the world is under this atheistic brutality means these people are not only forbidden freedom of religion, but they are prohibited from hearing an evangelist or missionary. The Iron Curtain shuts out the gospel as well as shuts in the enslaved people.

An amazing fact of history is that *church* leaders would turn to socialism as a means of achieving their religious goals. Socialism seeks to have the state control and distribute the goods of society. Thus the government becomes the force to implement religious programs.

The history of socialism can be traced to Europe. In 1825 Claude Henri Saint-Simon published a work called *The New Christianity*. It greatly influenced Karl Marx, who embraced the social gospel concept when he was seventeen years old, but he changed to atheistic communism later under the influence of the socialist, Baron Ludwig von Westphalen, who became his father-in-law.[4]

The goal of atheistic socialism is to do away with the evils of capitalistic, industrial society. This has attracted many clergymen who believe that society, rather than individuals, is the sinful element in the world. They believe man is not depraved but the victim of his wicked environment. Thus the selfish business owners (or capitalists) are the enemies of society. The industrial world (especially in the nineteenth century) was cruel and heartless, allowing child labor, unsanitary conditions and low wages. Socialism presented a means to challenge the evil society and reform its problems. Furthermore, socialism attracted these clergymen with its hope of *utopia* or the ideal community.

The forerunner of the social gospel concept seems to be William Ellery Channing. Influenced at Harvard University by the antichristian concepts coming out of the French Revolution, he began to espouse socialism by 1799.[5] As an Unitarian clergyman, his sermons appealed to those who welcomed his ethical teachings. He spoke "of a Christian social gospel that would meet the wants of the sick, the poor, the uneducated."[6] Channing also pioneered the theology of the Fatherhood of God and the dignity and perfectibility of human nature.[7] Thus the doctrine of the original sin of man was rejected.

Another important clergyman was Washington Gladden (1836–1918), who greatly influenced the Congregational church with his view on socialism as the answer to society's problems. He is often called the Father of the Social Gospel.[8]

A more illustrious preacher of the nineteenth century was Henry Ward Beecher.

> He set a pattern for sheer opportunism and political churchianity that is unique in the history of Christianity. He was the popularizer of theistic evolution, gradualist socialism and the social action emphasis in church activity. In 1871 Beecher echoed Karl Marx's support of the communist revolt of the Paris Commune and he prophesied a proletarian revolution in the United States.[9]

But it was a young New York pastor who popularized the social gospel with his books and lectures. Walter Rauschenbusch (1861–1918) was a socialist all his life. While ministering in poverty-stricken areas of New York City, he became convinced that socialism could solve the needs of these desperately poor people.

Other early social gospel leaders were Dwight Porter Bliss, who organized the Society of Christian Socialists, and Horace Bushnell, who originated the "new theology" or "progressive orthodoxy." Harnack, the Greek scholar; Richard Ely, professor of political economy at Johns Hopkins University; Graham Taylor, professor at Chicago Theological Seminary; Charles Sheldon, Methodist author of *In His Steps*; Shailer Matthew, Baptist dean of the Divinity School at the University of Chicago: These were important spokesmen in promoting the social gospel. In 1931 the Fellowship of Socialist Christians was organized by John C. Bennett and Reinhold Niebuhr of Union Theological Seminary.

Thus we see that the social gospel was strictly an American movement. These clergymen were revolting against Calvinism and Puritanism.[10]

As the main Protestant denominations turned from Biblical authority and historic Christianity to theological liberalism, the social gospel became the message and ministry of the church.

> The Christian social gospel gets whatever validity it has, not from any emphasis on altruism or even on respect for individual personality . . . but rather from the fact that it proposes to Christianize the world, not in atomistic fashion by changing individuals one at a time, but by refashioning the structure of human relationships, by the building of a spiritual community in which personality can grow. In other words, the social gospel proposes to synchronize individual and social redemption.[11]

Thus the social gospel rejects or at least minimizes individual sin and the need for individual conversion. It is applying the ethics of Christ to society while rejecting His Lordship and redemption. The Christ of the social gospel is not the Jesus Christ of the Bible; He is a fictional, mythical, humanist ideal which has been concocted by religious men (2 Cor. 11:4). Durant Drake, the noted liberal, stated:

> It is the spirit of Christ, the ministry of love and self-sacrifice, that is slowly lifting men upward; that event on Calvary, nineteen hundred years ago, symbolizes this age-

long process; the doctrine that has crystallized round it expresses in concrete and tangible form a profound and pathetic truth.[12]

So the Christ of the Bible to the advocate of the social gospel is symbolic and pictorial, not divine and not the Lamb of God Who bore the sins of mankind.

Many of the advocates of the social gospel did not necessarily reject personal conversion altogether. Walter Rauschenbusch claimed to believe in it. Jitsuo Morikawa, past secretary, Division of Evangelism, American Baptist Home Mission Society, and former pastor of the Riverside Drive Church, New York City, stated his view as a liberal:

> There is considerable feeling that we have confused evangelism and social action, by-passing evangelism in favor of social action. . . . Thus evangelism is the good news of something new, the newness of God in Jesus Christ erupting into history, His total activity of transforming the old into the New Creation (Rom. 8:19-23). . . . But God acts in different ways as He has in the past—events in history like the Exodus, Exile, Crucifixion, Resurrection; the word of the prophets and apostles; the witness of the community of Israel and the church. So today He continues to act through events in history, whether they be Civil Rights activities, international events, domestic social legislation, or some other event . . . and since action of God as well as the church is social (in relation to people), the least we can say is that social action is an important dimension of evangelism.[13]

The desired effect of the social gospel according to two of its popular advocates, Shailer Matthew in his book *The Individual and the Social Gospel* and Walter Rauschenbusch in his book *Christianizing the Social Order*, is to reform society by removing the evil elements and Christianizing it.[14] The social gospel, then, is the attempt to not only change social evil, but for men—through the church's influence along with the state and industry—to bring the "kingdom of God" on earth.

Most of this century's political movements have been based on the social gospel: Theodore Roosevelt's Square Deal, Wilson's New Freedom, Franklin Roosevelt's New Deal, and especially Lyndon Johnson's Great Society, which incorporated a host of civil rights and welfare programs into law.

Out of this social emphasis came the Federal Council of Churches, now named the National Council of Churches, and the World Council of Churches. These organizations support socialistic and communistic causes which not only violate Biblical doctrine but undermine traditional American institutions and free enterprise.

Today every mainline Protestant denomination and school of higher education is contaminated with theological liberalism which advocates the social gospel. These church groups have banded together in the ecumenical movement to bring about the socialist utopia.

One of the modern advocates of socialism for the church is Harvey Cox (liberal American Baptist) who predicts in his book *The Secular City* that society will be and should be religious without God.[15] Cox comments and compliments former President John F. Kennedy, who attended the Fabian Socialist School of Economics in London:

> We have yet to measure the enormous contribution made by the brief administration of John F. Kennedy to the desacralizing (sic) of American society. His election itself marked the end of Protestant cultural hegemony. . . . [He] made an indispensable contribution to the authentic and healthy secularization of our society.[16]

Roman Catholics have not escaped the socialist penetration into their ranks. Their "liberation theology" is really a form of Marxism. Ray Hundley states in his article "The Dangers of Liberation Theology":

> At the same time, a similar process of ferment and discussion took place among the area's Roman Catholic theologians at the Episcopal Conference of Latin America in 1968. They produced a document that analyzed many glaring problems in terms of Marxist philosophy and then pro-

claimed some of the basic beliefs of Liberation Theology. Although the Catholic Church has exerted considerable pressure since that time to suppress the liberationist movement, it is still strong and growing. The Pope's attempts at Puebla, Mexico, and later in Brazil to squelch the movement among priests and theologians have so far proved ineffective. Though Protestant theologians probably came up with the first primitive attempts at creating a theology of liberation, the Roman Catholics have now "taken the ball and run with it." It is now propagated in most major Protestant and Roman Catholic seminaries of Latin America.[17]

George Peters names some of the spokesmen for this diabolical, anti-Christian philosophy. He lists among the leaders Roman Catholic Archbishop Don Helder Camera (Brazil) and Gustavo Gutierrez, professor at the Catholic University in Lima, Peru. Peters comments, "These 'apostles of liberation' do not hide their indebtedness to Karl Marx. . . ."[18]

But socialism can only function when freedom is limited or denied. The socialistic state, which is controlled by an elite few, becomes the final authority on what is right and best for people; it cannot tolerate free thinking and freedom-loving people. The American free enterprise system must be destroyed and Bible-teaching churches must be stifled for socialism to function. This is the reason social gospel advocates support socialist politicians and are reluctant to admit the moral bankruptcy of the Soviet Russian empire. Politicians and clergymen are almost blind toward socialism's failures.

No wonder the liberal, socialistic New Deal philosophy of the Franklin Roosevelt regime recognized and aided the Soviet Union.[19] The U.S.S.R. is the socialists' ideal, the utopia, the dream fulfilled. This is why the unrealistic policies of the American government since World War II have fed, financed and armed this backward, barbaric country and its satellites. Socialist loyalties run deep.

Not only are the mainline Protestant churches socialist minded; many union leaders, much of the public school system, many university faculty members, plus the vast majority of politicians, economists, journalists and government advisors are either socialists or influenced by socialist training.[20] Socialism decries nationalism, balanced budgets, property ownership, the work ethic, and freedom of speech, worship and press. Socialism wants the overthrow of American democracy (the republic) by either revolution (communism) or by gradual control (Fabianism).

The American public, including fundamentalists, does not comprehend the influence that socialism has had on American political and educational life. The world-renowned English Fabian socialist, John Maynard Keynes, became the star economist of Harvard University in the 1930s. Walter Lippman was a member of the Harvard Board of Overseers during the complete sellout to socialism of the Harvard Economics Department (1933–1939). Harvard professor John Kenneth Galbraith and others have influenced many economists and politicians, and, sad to say, theologians.[21]

A tragic result of the social gospel is the rejection of preaching that the Christ Who died for sin and rose again is the only means of eternal salvation. Missions has become a "mission," and evangelism has become social action. Clyde Taylor quotes James De-Forrest Murch in his book *The World Council of Churches—An Analysis and Evaluation:*

> The International Missionary Conferences at Willingen (1952) marked the turning point from missions to mission. While using a cloak of Biblical words it (1) disowned an authoritative Bible, (2) made mission-theory God-centered rather than Christ-centered, (3) saw the cross as the fulfillment of God's missionary will and the creation of immovable realities in the course of world history, (4) saw the church as God's instrument in mission, and (5) accepted the establishment of God's kingdom—a redeemed society—as the mission of the church. Any such digest of the findings at Willingen is an oversimplification but it states the essential position of the ecumenical leaders. Many of these leaders see Christianity as the fulfillment rather than the contradiction of the non-Christian religions and show a readiness to emphasize "the good in all religions."[22]

Consequently, the worldwide conspiracy to break down traditions and freedoms is being accomplished by socialistic programs.

And the apostate church is one of the mightiest tools of Satan to fulfill this destruction.

One thing is certain: the fundamentalist repudiates the social gospel. Paul warned of a different gospel which was not another one (Gal. 1:6–8). He made it clear that another gospel was anathema!

Notes:

1. "Socialism: Trials and Errors," *Time* (March 13, 1978), 24.

2. Richard Wurmbrand, *Was Marx a Satanist?* (Glendale, CA: Diane Books, 1977), p. 12.

3. Ibid., p. 23.

4. Robert D. Hayden and Zygmund Dobbs, *The Social Gospel—Socialist Seduction of the Scriptures* (West Sayville, NY: Zygmund Dobbs, 1973), p. 15.

5. Ibid., p. 12.

6. Ibid., p. 13.

7. Alan H. Hamilton, "The Social Gospel, Part II," *Bibliotheca Sacra* (July—September 1951), 314.

8. Alan H. Hamilton, "The Social Gospel, Part III," *Bibliotheca Sacra* (October—December 1951), 475.

9. Hayden and Dobbs, p. 14.

10. Hamilton (July—September 1951), pp. 312–314.

11. Alan H. Hamilton, "The Social Gospel," *Bibliotheca Sacra* (April—June 1950), 215, quoting F. Ernest Johnson, *The Social Gospel Re-Examined*, p. 266.

12. Durant Drake, *The Problems of Religion* (New York: Houghton Mifflin Co., 1916), p. 178.

13. Jitsuo Morikawa, "Toward a Dialogue on Evangelism," (Valley Forge, PA: American Baptist Home Mission Society, n.d.), p. 3.

14. Hamilton (April—June 1950), p. 213.

15. Harvey Cox, *The Secular City* (New York: Macmillian Co., 1966), pp. 460, 461.

16. Ibid., p. 86.

17. Ray Hundley, "The Dangers of Liberation Theology," *Focus on Missions* (February 1982), 1.

18. George W. Peters, "Current Theological Issues in World Missions," *Bibliotheca Sacra* (April—June 1978), 162.

19. Lawrence L. Knutson, "A Horse Trade," *Houston Chronicle* (November 19, 1983).

20. Ralph C. Dean, "A U.S. Trend to Socialism?" *Des Moines Register* (April 26, 1971).

21. Zygmund Dobbs, *Keynes at Harvard* (West Sayville, NY: Probe Research, 1962), pp. 112, 113.

22. Clyde Taylor, "World Missions and the Ecumenical Movement," *The Coming World Church* (Lincoln, NE: Good News Broadcasting Assn., 1963), p. 38, quoting James DeForrest Murch, *The World Council of Churches—An Analysis and Evaluation*, p. 18.

5

The Cultural Mandate

The idea of the "cultural mandate" came out of old-line Reformed circles in Holland a generation ago. Its recent advocate is Herman Dooyeweerd, who was Professor of History and Philosophy of Law at the Free University in Amsterdam. His thesis is that believers have two commissions to fulfill. One is the Great Commission to evangelize individuals in all nations (Matt. 28:18–20), and the other commission is to evangelize the culture and structures of society, eventually to bring, by human effort, all nations under the sovereignty of Christ.[1]

This second mandate places the responsibility of social change on believers. They are to penetrate the structures of society and apply Christian principles to areas of labor, business, politics and education.

The Scriptural basis for this movement is Genesis 1:28: "And God blessed them, and God said unto them, Be fruitful, and multiply, and replenish the earth, and subdue it: and have dominion over the fish of the sea, and over the fowl of the air, and over every living thing that moveth upon the earth." The key word is "subdue." The advocates of the cultural mandate say this command is still in force as it was never abrogated. Further, a similar charge was given to Noah in Genesis 9:1, though the word "subdue" is not repeated.

Who are the advocates of this position? One is the "father" of new evangelicalism, Harold John Ockenga. As a matter of fact, he bestowed the honorary Doctor of Letters upon Dr. Dooyeweerd at the 1970 commencement at Gordon College.[2] Furthermore, Gordon College publicized the event along with pictures and an address by Senator Mark O. Hatfield, which dealt with this philosophy applied to current issues of war, race and poverty.

Dr. Ockenga was one of the pioneer rebels against fundamentalism. He stated in 1957:

> The New Evangelicalism differs from Fundamentalism in its willingness to handle the social problems which Fundamentalism evaded. . . . Fundamentalism abdicated leadership and responsibility in the societal realm and thus became impotent to change society or solve social problems.[3]

Another proponent of the cultural mandate is former professor at Dallas Theological Seminary, George Peters.[4] Another is Arthur Glasser of Fuller Seminary. He stated in *Freedom Now*:

> God holds men accountable for the course of civilization. They should insist on political integrity, ease racial tensions, improve housing standards, remove the causes of war, and ameliorate all forms of human suffering. A valid missionary strategy for the church dare not overlook or downgrade the cultural mandate. In our day, the conservative evangelical segment of the missionary movement is widely criticized for its truncated witness to Jesus Christ evidenced by its neglect of the cultural mandate. In my judgment there is much validity to this criticism. We tend to interpret the victory of Jesus almost exclusively in individualistic terms. Our theology fails to grapple with culture. Our ethic does not embrace the totality of human endeavor, particularly the cultural pursuit. We are preoccupied with non-cultural activities (prayer meetings, Bible studies, personal witness) and imply that God finds in them alone His will being done "on earth as it is in heaven."[5]

Dr. Glasser expressed his views in this interview conducted by *Eternity* magazine:

Petersen: What do you mean by the cultural mandate?
Glasser: Well, in Scripture there are two mandates: the

evangelistic mandate and the cultural mandate. Salvation really has the implications of both. According to the cultural mandate, God desires to involve men in accepting responsibility for the world. He is concerned about the poor, the oppressed, the weak. He is concerned about government, injustice, oppression and so on.

Petersen: Do you believe in a cultural mandate?

Glasser: I certainly do. . . . As an evangelical, I cannot stand against what the Bible says about my responsibility in relation to government, to war, to racism, and so forth. Just as the World Council has forgotten the evangelistic mandate, so evangelicals have forgotten the cultural mandate.[6]

Another advocate is Conservative Baptist missionary leader H. Walter Fricke, who clearly shared his cultural mandate philosophy in the March—April 1973 editorial in *Impact*:

"In addition to evangelizing and planting the church, historically missions have usually included the personal and social welfare of people. The task of the Church may be reproduction, but included in its mandate are literacy, education, literature, medicine, relief, orphanages, and widow and prison ministries. In economically depressed areas missions have introduced new methods of agriculture, industry and commerce, lifting the level of human dignity. Missionaries spear-headed social reform, public health, infant welfare, struck at slavery, raised the status of women and helped outlaw degrading practices. . . . The task of spiritual and social reform is not finished." He then called for a new wave of doctors, nurses, paramedics, clinics, educators, teachers, translators, journalists, authors—all who can make a contribution to "the spread and depth of Gospel penetration."[7]

What is wrong with the cultural mandate? Very simple! The command to Adam and Eve recorded in Genesis 1:28 was given *before the Fall*. "Subdue the earth" had to do with a perfect environment (no curse) which was just beginning to function and to be populated. Other than Genesis 9:1, which was given after the flood when the earth was empty and society was beginning again, there is no Scripture of support. Gentry attempts to support the cultural mandate from Hebrews 2:5-8, but he cannot. He also believes the "image of God" involves this command to dominate society, but he does not explain the crisis of the fall of Adam and its effect on the nature of man (Gen. 5:1-3).[8]

It is a mystery why Bible believers can build a whole system on such weak evidence. Unfortunately, the Christian church has been plagued too much and too often by such shoddy scholarship. Martin Lloyd-Jones makes clear the fallacy of the cultural mandate:

> You can't reform the world. That's why I disagree with the "social and cultural mandate" preaching and its appeal to Genesis 1:28. It seems to me to forget completely the Fall of man. You can't Christianize the world. The endtime is going to be like the time of the Flood.[9]

Bryce Augsburger has discerned the erroneous premise of the cultural mandate: "The Cultural Mandate is rooted in amillennialism which has eliminated any idea of a future kingdom and which must do its best with the kingdom here and now."[10]

Notes:

1. Bryce Augsburger, "The Cultural Mandate" (April 1980), p. 1.
2. G. Archer Weninger, "The Deadly Menace of the Cultural Mandate" (speech delivered to the Fundamental Baptist Fellowship, Denver, June 14, 1973), p. 2.
3. Ibid., p. 3.
4. Ibid., p. 4.
5. Ibid.
6. William J. Petersen, "What Evangelicals Can Learn from Bangkok," *Eternity* (April 1973), 27-29.
7. H. Walter Fricke, "The Crippling Faith," *Impact* (March—April 1973), 2.
8. Kenneth L. Gentry, Jr., "Bible Teaching on Civil Government, Part II," *The Christian Alternative* (December 1983), 2.
9. Carl F. H. Henry, "Martyn Lloyd-Jones: From Buckingham to Westminster," *Christianity Today* (February 8, 1980), 33, 34.
10. Augsburger, p. 5.

6

Reformed Theology

A correct view of eschatology (the doctrine of last things) is necessary if one is to correctly understand the future of society. Premillennialism holds that while this age will end in apostasy and tribulation, Christ will return to establish a one-thousand-year reign of righteousness. Both amillennialism and postmillennialism, while differing from each other in some aspects, do not believe the future final age will be Christ's reigning over society.

The historic position of Reformed (or Reformation) Theology has been postmillennialism. Only recently have reformed theologians held an amillennial position. (Reformation Theology is a system of Bible interpretation based on theological covenants. It results in confusion over the distinction of Israel and the church and over the purpose of the church.)

John Walvoord (a premillennialist) describes the postmillennial position toward changing society: ". . . That through preaching of the Gospel the whole world will be Christianized and brought to submission to the Gospel before the return of Christ. The name is derived from the fact that in this theory Christ returns after the Millennium."[1] Note that the church, through the power of the gospel, is to "Christianize" society. Thus the church, by the efforts of men, will change the world system to subdue sin and evil. The renowned Baptist theologian, Augustus Hopkins Strong (a postmillennialist), expressed it this way:

We may therefore best interpret Rev. 20:4–10 as teaching in highly figurative language, not a preliminary resurrection of the body, in the case of departed saints, but a period in the later days of the church militant when, under special influence of the Holy Ghost, the spirit of the martyrs shall appear again, true religion be greatly quickened and revived, and the members of Christ's churches become so conscious of their strength in Christ that they shall, to an extent unknown before, triumph over the powers of evil both within and without.[2]

Berkhof, a staunch amillennialist, points out that modern-day postmillennialists, such as social gospel advocate Walter Rauschenbusch, differ from the reformers and their disciples. Rauschenbusch believed that evolution would bring on the Millennium gradually because man would adopt a constructive policy of world betterment.[3] Berkhof rejects the idealist doctrine of changing society just before Christ returns to earth, as postmillennialism holds. He further states, "This Kingdom cannot be established by natural but only by supernatural means."[4] So there is a basic division even among reformed theologians.

The traditional postmillennial view has had many great students. Some of these are Charles Hodges, A. A. Hodges and Caspar Hodges (all of Princeton fame), W. G. T. Shedd, Robert L. Dabney, Henry B. Smith, Augustus H. Strong, Benjamin B. Warfield and, more recently, David Brown and Loraine Boettner.

Some of the Old Testament Scriptures postmillennialists use are Numbers 14:21; Psalms 47:2; 97:5; Isaiah 40:5; 49:6; Zechariah 9:10. Postmillennialists hold that "Christ teaches that society is to be transformed by the Kingdom of heaven, and the result will be a Christianized world."[5]

We find that Christ's work of redemption truly has as its object the people of the entire world and that His Kingdom is to become universal. And since nothing is told us as to how long the earth shall continue after that goal has been reached, possibly we can look forward to a great "golden age" of spiritual prosperity continuing for centuries, or even for millenniums, during which time Christianity shall be triumphant over all the earth, and during which time the great proportion even of adults shall be saved. It seems that the number of the redeemed shall then be swelled until it far surpasses that of the lost.

. . . .

The number of those who are saved may eventually bear some such proportion to those who are lost as the number of free citizens in our commonwealth today bears to those who are in the prisons and penitentiaries; or that the company of the saved may be likened to the main stalk of the tree which grows and flourishes, while the lost are but as the small limbs and prunings which are cut off and which are destroyed in the fires. This is the prospect that Postmillennialism is able to offer. Who even among those holding other systems would not wish that it were true?[6]

So then postmillennialism believes the world is gradually growing better and that righteousness will prevail. Postmillennialists are careful to point out that individual conversions are the means to accomplish this goal and that sin will not be eradicated. According to them, Christianity is increasing its influence, and modern civilization is flourishing under the shadow of the church. Knowledge, justice, Bible teaching, spiritual and moral life are all improving society. This change is perhaps very gradual but truly there. Boettner sums up his dream and hope with these words:

Thus Postmillennialism holds that Christianity is to become the controlling and transforming influence not only in the moral and spiritual life of some individuals, but also in the entire social, economic and cultural life of the nations. There is no reason why this change should not take place over the entire earth, with pagan religions and false philosophies giving place to the true, and the earth being restored in considerable measure to that high purpose of righteousness and holiness for which it was created.[7]

One of the main propositions of postmillennialists to support their view that the church is "Christianizing" society is their interpretation of the parable of Jesus on the leaven found in Matthew 13. To them, the leaven is the gospel and the meal is the human race. Boettner states:

The parable of the leaven teaches the universal extension and triumph of the Gospel, and it further teaches that this development is accomplished through the gradual development of the Kingdom, not through a sudden and cataclysmic explosion. . . . Society is to be transformed by the Kingdom of heaven, and the result will be a Christianized world.[8]

How does this idealist interpretation of both the Scriptures and the trends in society hold up under the facts? Not well. Fact: The world is certainly not improving. Moral degradation, the threat of nuclear war, the increase of paganism and apostasy, and the declining influence of evangelical churches just do not support the postmillennial ideal.

Fact: The Scriptures clearly teach that this age will end in apostasy, not revival (2 Tim. 3:1–7; et al.). Furthermore, Jesus stated that "few" would be saved and "many" would be lost (Matt. 7:13, 14). The entire book of Revelation sets forth a pessimistic picture of catastrophe, apostasy and the reign of antichrist before Christ returns.

Furthermore, the presumptions of postmillennialism give impetus to those who support the social gospel. Also the teaching that the kingdom of God will be realized on earth through human efforts parallels the Roman Catholic view originally set forth by Augustine.[9]

Amillennialism harms the cause of Christ by giving emphasis to the visible church, which to the amillennialist is the center of God's program.[10]

When the literal method of hermeneutics is consistently followed, the Old Testament promises yet unfulfilled are understood as still on God's prophetic calendar. The reformed theological practice of "spiritualizing" Scripture on eschatology has provided an unfortunate view, not only of Israel and the world, but also of the church of Jesus Christ. The only consistent and comprehensive approach to understanding God's purpose, plan and power is to hold to the premillennial interpretation of Christ's return.

W. E. Blackstone in his monumental book, *Jesus Is Coming*, sums up the issues with this comparison:

Post-millennialists seem to think that all must be accomplished under the Church, and with present instrumentalities.

Pre-millennialists look for the main accomplishment under Christ Himself, who will cut short the work in righteousness, and with different instrumentalities.

Post-millennialism exalts the Church.

Pre-millennialism exalts Jesus and fills the heart of the believer with a LIVING, PERSONAL, COMING Savior.

Post-millennialists, though ACKNOWLEDGING that the Second Advent of Christ is the very POLE STAR of the Church, have little heart in it. This is natural and perfectly consistent for those who believe the event is at least a thousand years away.

They very seldom preach or talk about it.[11]

Notes:

1. John F. Walvoord, "The Millennial Issue in Modern Theology," *Bibliotheca Sacra* (January—March 1949), 45.

2. Augustus Hopkins Strong, *Systematic Theology* (Philadelphia: Judson Press, 1907), p. 1013.

3. Louis Berkhof, *Systematic Theology* (Grand Rapids: Wm. B. Eerdmans, 1946), p. 717.

4. Ibid., p. 719.

5. Loraine Boettner, *The Millennium* (Philadelphia: Presbyterian and Reformed, 1958), p. 27.

6. Ibid., pp. 29, 35.

7. Ibid., p. 53.

8. Ibid.

9. J. Dwight Pentecost, *Things to Come* (Findlay, OH: Dunham Publishing Co., 1958), p. 387.

10. Ibid., p. 388.

11. W. E. Blackstone, *Jesus Is Coming* (New York: Fleming H. Revell, 1908), pp. 114, 115.

7

New
Evangelicalism

New evangelicalism arrived on the religious scene after World War II as a revolt against fundamentalism. One of its key spokesmen was Harold John Ockenga, who coined the word in 1957. He stated in 1960:

> Time revealed certain weaknesses in the fundamentalist cause. First was the diversion of strength from the great offensive work of missions, evangelism, and Christian education to the defense of the faith. The fundamentalists were maneuvered into the position of holding the line against the constant and unremitting attacks of the modernists or liberals. Gradually the liberals took over the control of the denominations and began a series of acts of discrimination, ostracism, and persecution of the evangelicals. Many evangelicals suffered at the hands of ecclesiastical modernism. This reduced fundamentalism to a holding tactic, impotent in denominational machinery and indifferent to societal problems rising in the secular world. The Christian Reformed Church was a notable exception to this trend. The cause of the fundamentalist defeat in the ecclesiastical scene lay partially in fundamentalism's erroneous doctrine of the Church which identified the Church with believers who were orthodox in doctrine and separatist in ethics. Purity of the Church was emphasized above the peace of the Church. Second Corinthians 6:14–17 was used to justify the continuous process of fragmentation, contrary to the meaning of the passage itself.[1]

He stated in a news release on December 8, 1957:

> The New Evangelicalism is the latest dress of orthodoxy
> as Neo-Orthodoxy is the latest expression of theological
> liberalism. The New Evangelicalism differs from Fundamen-
> talism in its willingness to handle the social problems which
> Fundamentalism evaded. There need be no dichotomy
> between the personal gospel and the social gospel. The true
> Christian faith is a supernatural personal experience of
> salvation and a social philosophy. Doctrine and social ethics
> are Christian disciplines. Fundamentalism abdicated leader-
> ship and responsibility in the societal realm and thus became
> impotent to change society or to solve social problems. The
> New Evangelicalism adheres to all the orthodox teachings
> of Fundamentalism but has evolved a social philosophy.[2]

This viewpoint expressed by Dr. Ockenga is a radical change
from his previous position. In 1948 he repudiated those who advocated social action. He lamented:

> Ours is a time of deflection from the primary to the
> secondary emphasis of the church. Our day emphasizes the
> ecumenical movement rather than the evangelical convic-
> tion of Christianity. . . . Social betterment rather than
> evangelism is the program for the day. The church is
> substituting legislative power for the spiritual power. Cer-
> tainly the church ought to be interested in all efforts for
> good, but more playgrounds do not make better children.[3]

So among other vital areas of Biblical truth, the new evangelical
sharply criticizes and pointedly departs from the fundamentalist
over social responsibilities. According to these critics, the fundamentalist has failed to do his duty. He is letting the world go to hell
while he waits for the rapture! It is a "tragic cop-out; in fact, an
active hindrance to the fulfillment of Christian social responsibility."[4]

Senator Mark Hatfield, an influential new evangelical, shares
his views on social responsibility and how he was affected by Carl
F. H. Henry, who led the repudiation of fundamentalism:

I cite these examples not to maintain that our social and political attitudes should remain severed from biblical perspectives. On the contrary, I believe the evangelical community has as its most urgent task the developing of a responsible social and political ethic that takes with equal seriousness both the truth of Christ's life and God's revelation of himself to man and the crises confronting the social and political institutions of our age.

Carl F. H. Henry noted this fact in his volume entitled *The Uneasy Conscience of Modern Fundamentalism*. Dr. Henry pointed out that the gospel was for the *whole* man—questions pertaining to the reconciliation between God and man could not be separated from questions pertaining to the reconciliation between man and his fellow-man.

Dr. Henry maintained that the religious liberals had upset this balance by emphasizing human relations to such an extent that they lost sight of the theological basis upon which reconciliation occurs. At the same time, however, Dr. Henry argued that conservatives had upset this balance in the opposite direction. They were so obsessed with maintaining the spiritual and religious dogmas of the orthodox credo that they lost sight of its ethical implications and imperatives. Along with others, Henry urged the conservative theological community to rethink its obligations to the social sphere.[5]

The new evangelicals seem to be embarrassed by the prosperity of America. They gravitate to liberal politics, ecumenical programs and mainline church denominations. They base their social concern on the needs of the world and on their concepts of theology, not on the direct teachings of Scripture. They expound on love, justice and goodness as attributes of God and so conclude Christians should endeavor to change the evils of the world system. Carl Henry expresses this kind of logic in his book *Aspects of Christian Social Ethics* with this insight on new-evangelical thinking:

Christian doctrine is a harmonious unity whose main axis is the nature of God. For this reason a correct understanding of the whole range of Christian faith and duty turns on a proper comprehension of divine attributes. How the theologian defines and relates God's sovereignty, righteousness, and love actually predetermines his exposition of basic positions in many areas—in social ethics. . . .[6]

Another motivation to the new evangelical is the kingdom of God. He would reject the liberal view of the social gospel's kingdom, but nonetheless he desires to bring its influence to bear on social evils. Mott states his new-evangelical view:

> We receive the Reign as a gift but with it comes a demand and the power to meet that demand so that we can be channels of God's creation. The Reign of God is not social program, but faithfulness to its demands for justice necessitates social programs and social struggle. The Reign, which shows up the relativity of such efforts, also provides the motivation and grace to carry them out.
> Social action in service to God who is creating the Reign is not a matter of human arrogance. It is the obedient and joyful use of the powers that God has given us in Christ. It is faithfulness in the opportunities that God has opened up to us in God's long march through the history of the peoples, and powers, and institutions that form the kingdom which God will not give up.[7]

Mott articulates the new-evangelical view that the Christian's responsibility in social concern extends beyond believers in need. He attempts to show that "brother" (1 John 4:20; 3:17) and "saints" (2 Cor. 8:4) speak of the larger society of men, not just believers.

> Therefore to be consistent and faithful to the whole of Scripture and particularly to be true to these teachings of Jesus, we would have to generalize and universalize the teachings of I John, II Corinthians 8 and 9, and Matthew 25 and see them as material for social ethics. They become a standard and example of the love which we must apply to all people. . . . But if the question of the larger sphere of responsibility were raised, *brother* or *sister* could be replaced by *fellow-man* or *fellow-woman*.[8]

Mott argues that the phrases "to all" and "for all" (1 Thess. 3:12; 5:15) should obligate the Christian to include the whole world—not just the Christian community—in his good works. Surely such general admonitions from the Apostle do not give instructions to the church of Thessalonica to attack the social structures of society and to take on the care of the city's (and the world's) poor and downtrodden. The fact is that there is no indication the apostolic church practiced social activity at all!

Mott's style and burden is commendable in that he is genuinely concerned for the needy of society. But his exegesis is wanting. He just does not have clear, sound doctrinal support from the Bible. It is similar to Carl Henry's books on Christian social involvement. Dr. John Walvoord leveled just criticism on Carl Henry when he reviewed his book, *Aspects of Christian Social Ethics:* "While it is impossible always to tie modern situations to specific Scriptural texts, his discussion might have been strengthened if his occasional treatment of Scriptures bearing on social ethics had been extended and made more explicit."[9]

This is really the issue! There are just not the Bible instructions nor the examples to warrant the new-evangelical passion for social involvement. Of course, there are injustices and inequities in the world, and people hurt, are hungry and are harrassed. Believers should and do feel for these victims. But fundamentalists rightly declare that helping unsaved individuals who need charity, whether it be out of kindness or for evangelistic reasons, it is not evangelism, nor is it fulfilling the commission of Christ. Deeds of love and acts of kindness are normal actions of compassionate Christians, but this does not justify reforming the world system!

Richard Quebedeaux, who is the author of *The Young Evangelicals* and proponent of the radical view of new evangelicalism, quotes David Moberg's book, *The Great Reversal: Evangelism versus Social Concern:*

> In regard to most social issues of this century, evangelicals are known for their negative positions—what they are against—rather than for a positive stand. They have worked for changed lives of individuals but not for changes in society, except as these might incidentally occur through converts. At the same time, they have described social conditions as going from bad to worse without recognizing that their own lack of social action to correct the structural evils of society and their professed "neutrality," which in reality

constituted support of the power structure, were major factors contributing to the deterioration of social conditions.[10]

Quebedeaux claims the young evangelicals espouse a truly evangelical social gospel. He ridicules the fundamentalist and chides the new evangelical as inconsistent. He states the priorities of the young evangelicals' social concern as "(1) sexual love as a joyful experience; (2) meaningful interpersonal and social relationships and the dignity of women; (3) racial justice; (4) the politics of conscience; (5) the fight against poverty; (6) a healthy natural environment; and (7) a positive and happy participation in contemporary culture."[11]

So the new evangelical opens the gate to all sorts of goals. It is a conformity to this age, not separation (Rom. 12:2). His gospel takes on a dual purpose which includes social causes. Mott describes the value of evangelism to social matters with these views:

> The contribution of conversion and consequently of evangelism to social change comes not only through God's provision of gracious power to help others, but also through the satisfaction of the personal need for healing in the center of our being . . . and by a new direction in social relationships.[12]

While Dr. Mott puts evangelism and social action on a parity, others include social action as part of the gospel. Dr. Donn Ketcham warns of this view, held by such noted scholars as John R. W. Stott:

> A great deal of interest is being placed on another view of the relationship between evangelism and social action. The primary spokesman for this point of view is John R. W. Stott, the Rector Emeritus of All Souls Church in London. Stott has been identified with the evangelical movement and has been one of her favorite spokesmen. There was a time when Stott felt that "the mission of the church, according to the specification of the risen Lord, is exclusively a preaching, converting and teaching mission." Over a period of time, Stott has changed his view. He held the above view in 1966. By 1975 he was saying, "Today, how-

ever, I would express myself differently . . . I now see more clearly that not only the consequences of the (Great) commission, but the actual commission itself must be understood to include social as well as evangelistic responsibility. . . ." His view is that it is not that we are to do all that Jesus commanded and social responsibility is *among* our mandates, but that social action is raised to be an actual part of the Great Commission along side of, and on a plane with, evangelism.[13]

Further warning comes from Ernest Pickering, author of several articles and books on the compromise of new evangelicals. He evaluates the trends of the new-evangelical philosophy with the following:

More and more radical views regarding social involvement are proceeding from professedly evangelical sources. Professor Wells, a teacher at Calvin College, sees the responsibility of the church to be "leaven for society" and justifies the young evangelicals for "joining the liberals in causes of social concern" ("Where My Generation Parts Company," *Eternity*, May 1970). These contemporary evangelicals have gone so far that many of them are now claiming that the call to social action is actually part of the gospel of Christ.[14]

In 1982 The Consultation on the Relationship between Evangelism and Social Responsibility met at Grand Rapids, Michigan, to grapple with the purpose of the Great Commission. Does evangelism include social action? This conference was sponsored by the World Evangelical Fellowship and the Lausanne Committee for World Evangelism. It was attended by forty-two participants and ten consultants from twenty-seven countries. Leaders included Leighton Ford (Billy Graham Association), Wade Coggins and Bruce Nicholls (WEF), John R. W. Stott and Ed Dayton (World Vision), Harold Lindsell (editor emeritus of *Christianity Today*) and John Perkins (black evangelist).

The major report of forty pages centered on social justice and its relationship to evangelism. Three kinds of "evangelism-social responsible relationship" were identified: social responsibility as a *consequence* of evangelism, social action as a *bridge* to evangelism, and social concern as a *partner* to evangelism.[15]

The dangers of this new-evangelical mixture of social action with evangelism are evident. Soon the two merge into one message; the purpose of missions becomes clouded, and ecclesiastical separation is totally rejected because programs take priority rather than doctrine. The apostle Paul warned of those who substituted earthly, social and materialistic priorities ahead of the spiritual ministry of the heavenly citizenship who look for the return of Christ to take Christians out of the decadent world. These who mind earthly things are enemies of the cross (Phil. 3:17–21).

The warning of the late Paul Jackson toward new evangelicals should be noted by every believer.

> One of the dangers [facing the church today] is the potential invasion of New Evangelicalism. I believe that the root of New Evangelicalism is a desire for the approval of men rather than the approval of God. We must not conform our interpretation of the Word of God to the current opinions of scientists, scholars, and philosophers when this compromises the evident teaching of God's Word. Intellectual achievement and discipline are a strength to be desired by anyone, as long as there is primary subjection to the Word of God, for the "fear of the LORD is the beginning of wisdom. . . ." Genuine fear of God will enable us to secure a thorough education without involvement in spiritual compromise. Education for a Christian should be a tool to intensify the effectiveness of his life for his Savior. It should not be an objective in itself.
>
> It is my prayer . . . that the GARBC will be aware of New Evangelicalism, for it is the greatest threat to the local church that has occurred in the twentieth century.[16]

Notes:

1. Harold John Ockenga, "Resurgent Evangelical Leadership," *Christianity Today* (October 10, 1960), 12.

2. William E. Ashbrook, "The New Neutralism," (Columbus, OH: Calvary Bible Church, 1966), p. 4, quoting Harold John Ockenga, News Release, December 8, 1957.

3. Harold John Ockenga, "The New Reformation," *Bibliotheca Sacra* (January—March 1948), 94, 95.

4. Lee Nash, "Evangelism and Social Concern," *The Cross and the Flag* (Carol Stream, IL: Creation House, 1972), p. 134.

5. Mark O. Hatfield, *Conflict and Conscience* (Waco, TX: Word Books, 1972), p. 24.

6. Charles C. Ryrie, "Perspectives on Social Ethics, Part I," *Bibliotheca Sacra* (January—March 1977), 35, quoting Carl F. H. Henry, *Aspects of Christian Social Ethics* (Grand Rapids: Wm. B. Eerdmans, 1964), p. 146.

7. Mott, *Biblical Ethics and Social Change,* p. 106.

8. Ibid., pp. 35, 36.

9. John F. Walvoord, "Book Reviews," *Bibliotheca Sacra* (October—December 1964), 316.

10. Quebedeaux, *The Young Evangelicals,* p. 101, quoting David Moberg, *The Great Reversal: Evangelism versus Social Concern* (Philadelphia: Lippincott, 1972), p. 177.

11. Ibid, pp. 101, 102.

12. Mott, p. 110.

13. Ketcham, *The World Hurts!* p. 11.

14. Ernest D. Pickering, *The Fruit of Compromise: The New and Young Evangelicals* (Clarks Summit, PA: Baptist Bible College of Pennsylvania, n.d.), p. 22.

15. Arthur P. Williamson, "The Great Commission or the Great Commandment?" *Christianity Today* (November 26, 1982), 36.

16. Craig Massey, "God's Man in the G.A.R.B.C." *Conquest* (April 2, 1967).

III

Responsibility
of the
Church

"But if I tarry long, that thou mayest know how thou oughtest to behave thyself in the house of God, which is the church of the living God, the pillar and ground of the truth" (1 Timothy 3:15).

8

The Intention
of the
Church

Before the nature and the purpose of the Church of Jesus Christ can be understood, the world system or age in which it ministers must be analyzed. Paul described this age as evil: "Who gave himself for our sins, that he might deliver us from this present evil world [age], according to the will of God and our Father" (Gal. 1:4); "Wherefore take unto you the whole armour of God, that ye may be able to withstand in the evil day, and having done all, to stand" (Eph. 6:13).

John identified society with the word "world": "Love not the world, neither the things that are in the world. If any man love the world, the love of the Father is not in him. For all that is in the world, the lust of the flesh, and the lust of the eyes, and the pride of life, is not of the Father, but is of the world. And the world passeth away, and the lust thereof: but he that doeth the will of God abideth for ever" (1 John 2:15–17).

The world system is society functioning in a rebel manner against God and His laws.

What, then, should the church be like? Its very meaning is significant, for it is *ecclesia* or called-out ones. The word was used in the Old Testament Greek translation, the Septuagint, for the nation of Israel when isolated in the wilderness. It also was the word for the government of the Greek city-states, where it identified the citizens who were qualified to vote. In Acts 19:39 the word translated "assembly" is *ecclesia*, identifying the citizens of Ephesus.

When *ecclesia* is translated "church," it means a body of individuals who have been *called out* of this wicked society. Its members must be regenerated by the Holy Spirit. A Biblical definition of a New Testament church is: ". . . A body of believers immersed upon credible confession of faith in Jesus Christ, having two officers (pastor and deacon), sovereign in polity, and banded together for work, worship, the observance of the ordinances, and the world-wide proclamation of the gospel."[1]

The discerning Bible student makes a clear distinction between Israel as God's Old Testament people and the church. Paul R. Jackson summarized the doctrine of the church with these words:

> The Church was purposed in the mind of God throughout the eternal ages; it was pictured in the Old Testament; it was promised by Jesus Christ during His earthly ministry; and it was purchased on the cross of Calvary. It was not produced, however, as a living reality until the Day of Pentecost, fifty days after the resurrection of Christ.[2]

When the line of distinction between regenerated people and religious people is broken down, confusion sets in. Not only is the church confused, but its place in society is confused. Friendship with the world should be rejected (James 4:4). Jesus prayed, "I have given them thy word; and the world hath hated them, because they are not of the world, even as I am not of the world" (John 17:14). And He warned His disciples, "If ye were of the world, the world would love his own: but because ye are not of the world, but I have chosen you out of the world, therefore the world hateth you" (John 15:19).

A study of the New Testament reveals the mission of the church to be (1) evangelism—winning the lost; (2) edification—building the saints; (3) apologetics—defending the faith. William Ditty summarizes the church's mission as (1) declaring the gospel; (2) discipling the saved; (3) defending the faith.[3] Nowhere do the Scriptures teach that the church as an organization should reform society, change the evil function of government, rescue the starving host of unfortunate people, or attack the injustices of the world. Fundamentalists have historically rejected social reform as the mission of the church.

In our day, however, a new voice of fundamentalism has arisen: Jerry Falwell and his associates. In his *Fundamentalist Journal*

(September 1982), Dr. Falwell rejected historical fundamentalism which has defended the faith against theological liberalism. According to him, this battle is past; fundamentalism today is evangelism and building super churches.

What about *social* involvement? Falwell's associates, Ed Dobson and Ed Hindson, wrote in the article, "The Church in the World and against the World":

> As we move into this new era, every element of our society is being challenged to justify its role in the shaping of the American dream. While some people tenaciously cling to the tradition of the past and others embrace the prospect of the new, the question must be asked: What should be the role of the church in society? . . . The ultimate role of the church must then transcend the very culture in which it exists. While maintaining its mission within the culture, it must also transform that culture by the gospel of Jesus Christ. . . .
>
> [The Christian] finds himself torn between the competing interests of the celestial and the terrestrial and therefore cannot passively function in any society. He must prophetically address the world in which he lives. There are several ways in which this can be done.
> 1. *Evangelism.* . . .
> 2. *Civil Obedience.* . . .
> 3. *Social Concern.* . . .
> 4. *Pluralism* [all religions are free and equal]. . . .
> 5. *Personal Testimony.* . . .
> The role of prophetic consciousness expresses itself in the following ways.
> 1. *Voting.* . . .
> 2. *Lobbying.* . . .
> 3. *Boycotting.* . . .
> 4. *Demonstrating.* . . .
> 5. *Resisting.* . . .
> In the past, Fundamentalists have emphasized only the preaching of the gospel, while Evangelicals [i.e., new evangelicals] have called for more social concern. Liberals have actually attempted to change society by aggressive social and political programs without the gospel. . . . Content to retreat to their spiritual "fortresses," Fundamentalists have

generally neglected the social and political process altogether. The time has come when we can no longer have
concern without action, change without conversion, or
social agenda without theological truth.

The role of the church in these complex and changing
times must ever be the same as it has always been—the
salt of the earth and the light of the world. We must first
call people to Christ, who alone can change them. We must
work to correct the injustices of an immoral and ungodly
society. We must be willing to confront evil with the courage of our convictions regardless of the cost. May God help
us to do it![4]

Dr. Falwell's purpose for the church has a *social* ministry. On
December 23, 1982, Dr. Falwell appeared on "Nightline" (the ABC
late-night news program) along with the Reverend Jesse Jackson
(Operation Push) and Father Charles Woodrich (Samaritan Shelter). The subject was churches helping the poor. Dr. Falwell stated:

> . . . There are 400,000 churches and synagogues in this
> country, and as Billy Graham said recently—and I think
> Senator Hatfield as well—if each church on the average
> could simply adopt 10 families, and realizing that some
> cannot do that much and some can do a great deal more,
> we would very much move into that vacuum [of
> government dropping help for the poor]. . . . We have 200
> of our young people from Lynchburg who are working
> in the inner cities. We're seeing in a practical way [what]
> all 400,000 churches can do. . . . We have 600 families with
> which we are working in Lynchburg. . . . But if we
> [churches] can on the average handle 10 families each, we
> can wipe out those persons' needs that are on public as-
> sistance. . . .
> I do feel that conservative churches 50 years ago, in the
> big struggle that went on here between liberalism and con-
> servatism in theological circles, that many of us in the con-
> servative area threw the baby out with the wash. We were
> so against the social gospel that we did not believe that
> we should do anything but preach the gospel of Christ,
> and we mustn't forget that. But at the same time, we're
> to feed the hungry and care for those who are needy, and
> we haven't—in our camp we accept the blame.[5]

Here is a leading fundamentalist personally blaming himself *as a fundamentalist* for not getting involved in social responsibilities sooner. He even has his local church feeding the community of Lynchburg, Virginia, and he desires all fundamentalist churches to incorporate social programs for their communities.

These views are quite different from what Falwell stated in 1965:

> Nowhere are we commissioned to reform the externals. . . . Our ministry is not reformation but transformation. The Gospel does not clean up the outside but rather regenerates the inside. . . . I would find it impossible to stop preaching the pure saving gospel of Jesus Christ and begin doing anything else including fighting communism, or participating in civil rights reform.[6]

Now Dr. Falwell wants social action. His Moral Majority has outlined a program of social action, namely, the saving of America. How? By uniting conservative Americans—of any or no religious persuasion—to reform this nation through the political process. This may be a noble goal, but *it is not Biblical truth.* There can be *no morality without spirituality!*

A host of new-evangelical men support Falwell. One of these is Sherwood Eliot Wirt who states in *The Social Conscience of the Evangelical*:

> If the Church shirks her duty to show the application of the Christian faith to the social needs of men, she does it at the expense of the good name of Christ in the world. . . . There is an increasing awareness on the part of evangelicals that the relationship of mission and social concern is made doubly important by the revolutionary nature of the times in which we live.[7]

Another critic of fundamentalism is Douglas Webster, writing in *Christianity Today*. Without much logic and no Scripture he advocates:

To glorify God, we must proclaim the gospel and care for the needy. We must condemn personal as well as societal sin. We must make the way of redemption plain as we seek justice for the oppressed. Evangelism and social action are equal partners; each is an end in itself, but Christ is the reason for both. Faithfulness to Christ means obedience in both areas.[8]

Still another critic, a prominent name in new-evangelical circles, is Ronald J. Sider. Dr. Sider claims social justice is neglected because evangelicals do not pay sufficient attention to Scripture. He boldly states:

Social concern involves both relief of those suffering from social injustice and the restructuring of all of society, saved and unsaved, for the sake of greater social justice. . . . I have argued both that evangelism and social concern are distinct and that they are inseparable. . . . [Evangelists] have failed to add that coming to Jesus ought necessarily to involve repentance of and conversion from the sin of involvement in social evils such as economic injustice and institutionalized racism. . . . Hence biblical social action will contain, always implicitly and often explicitly, a call to repentance. . . . That fact that evangelism and social concern are inseparable certainly does not mean that they are identical. They are distinct, equally important parts of the total mission of the church.[9]

Dr. Sider stresses the life of Christ as the model for believers today. While Jesus is truly the perfect example, careful interpretation of Scripture is necessary. Certainly Jesus performed marvelous miracles, but were these patterns for the church to emulate? The fact is these miracles were performed to declare and prove His Messianic credentials.

The passage which Dr. Sider believes is the key to the church's commitment to social concern is Luke 4:18 and 19. But this passage is quoted from Isaiah and applies to Jesus as the Messiah! Such unfortunate exegesis is demeaning of a professor in a Bible college. Dr. Sider dogmatizes: "The Gospels provide no indication that

Jesus considered healing sick people any less important than preaching the Good News. He commanded us both to feed the hungry
and to preach the Gospel."[10]

Sider reminds his critics of the liberal and Jewish interpretation of Jesus and His ministry, but he falls into the pit of prejudice
himself. Ryrie exposes the limited and erroneous viewpoint that
the ethical teaching of Jesus is paramount; he quotes the Jewish
scholar, J. Klausner, "The main strength of Jesus lay in his ethical
teaching."[11] Ryrie also exposes the heretical views of the liberal
Georgia Harkness, who holds Jesus only produced worthwhile
ethics not an authoritative Christ with the revelation of God.[12]

Dr. Ryrie carefully analyzes the teachings of Jesus on poverty,
wealth, duties, loving one's neighbor, feeding brethren and
priorities. One of his conclusions is that Jesus did not help
everyone! He did not heal everyone, nor feed all who were hungry,
nor attempt to reform the Roman government, nor settle legal
disputes and injustices among the Jews. His priority was spiritual
not material. Ryrie concludes his article:

> . . .Though not insensitive to physical needs, He minis-
> tered to relatively few of them. Though always obedient
> to government, He led no attempt to reform the system.
> Though capable of correcting all injustices in the social
> order, His message was a call to personal repentance.
> These were His perspectives on social ethics.[13]

The example of Jesus' earthly ministry can hardly be the prec-
edent for the church to reform the world. Jesus did not challenge
the injustice of Roman tyranny; He even paid the taxes laid on
Him and the disciples, "lest we should offend them" (Matt. 17:27).
While He did drive out the money-changers from the temple, this
appears to be more for spiritual than social or political reasons.
He did submit to the trial of the Sanhedrin and to Pilate and Herod.

Concerning the poor, Jesus acknowledged that poverty was
inevitable: "You have the poor with you always" (Mark 14:7). He
criticized wealthy men, not because of their abundance, but because
they trusted in it. In the culture of that day, wealth indicated God's
blessing; therefore, people sought wealth. Jesus repudiated this erroneous philosophy with, "Take heed, and beware of covetousness:

for a man's life consisteth not in the abundance of the things which he possesseth" (Luke 12:15). Jesus warned about the difficulty for rich people to be saved (Matt. 19:23, 24). But He did not scorn riches, wealth, education or authority. Nor did He settle all the evils and injustices of the society in which He lived. Ernest Pickering gives an accurate account of Jesus' ministry when he notes:

> . . . Christ could have undertaken a campaign to abolish poverty, but He did not. He presented the riches of His grace to the poor.
>
> He was concerned about the hungry (John 6:1–14), but He emphasized the spiritual bread which alone can satisfy (John 6:26, 27). Many of our Lord's mighty miracles were performed on outcasts and the needy of society (cf. John 9:1–7; Luke 17:11–19).[14]

The conclusion to Sider's premise that social concern is included in the purpose of the church cannot be supported from the Biblical accounts of the life of Jesus. But what about the apostolic church? Did the apostles practice social reform, and did they teach it in their epistles?

The believers' responsibility to society can be summed up by one word: *witness*. One can search in vain to locate examples or exhortations for the church to change social structures or to reform social evils. The church has a social responsibility to provide material support for preachers (1 Cor. 9:14; Gal. 6:6), widows (1 Tim. 5:3–10), orphans (James 1:27), poor saints in times of famine (Acts 11:27–30; Rom. 15:25; 2 Cor. 8, 9), and believers in need (1 John 3:17, 18). Believers are to work in the world (2 Thess. 3:12; 1 Tim. 5:8), live godly in society (Phil. 2:15, 16), pray for and obey unsaved secular authorities (Rom. 13:1–5; Titus 3:1), honor legal rulers (1 Pet. 2:17), give honest and honorable labor (1 Tim. 6:1), establish godly homes (Titus 2:1–10), refrain from giving offense to any (1 Cor. 10:31, 32), but attempt to win all to the saving knowledge of Christ (1 Cor. 10:33). Furthermore, in the Christian community redemption and spirituality are not limited by sex, race or social station (Col. 3:11; Gal. 3:28).

Believers are not to be conformed or fashioned by society (Rom. 12:2) nor to love it (1 John 2:15); they are to live peacefully and honestly in it (Rom. 12:17, 18). Yet there are specific occasions when obedience to God takes precedence over society's demands (Acts 5:29). Christians can appeal to legal authorities for protection of their rights as citizens (Acts 22:25; 25:11).

Nowhere does the New Testament relate or instruct the church to establish the Messianic Kingdom on earth or to Christianize society. The noted English pastor Martyn Lloyd-Jones comments, "I believe the Christian people—but not the church—should be involved in politics and in social affairs. The Kingdom task of the church is to save men from the wrath to come by bringing them to Christ." [15]

This distinction between the ministry of the church and that of individual believers is vital to understanding our stewardship in society. Therefore, the next subject to consider in the responsibility of the church is the responsibility of individual believers.

Notes:

1. L. Duane Brown, *Biblical Basis for Baptists* (North Ridgeville, OH: D & B Reproduction Service, 1983), p. 15.

2. Paul R. Jackson, *The Doctrine and Administration of the Church* (Schaumburg, IL: Regular Baptist Press, 1980), p. 19.

3. William Ditty, "The Mission of the Church," *Keystone Baptist* (January 1984), 1.

4. Ed Dobson and Ed Hindson, "The Church in the World and against the World," *Fundamentalist Journal* (July/August, 1983), 10, 11.

5. "Nightline" Transcript (December 23, 1982), 4–6.

6. *Blu-Print* (April 4, 1981), 1.

7. Wirt, *The Social Conscience of the Evangelical*, p. 151.

8. Douglas D. Webster, "Social Action Begins in the Local Church," *Christianity Today* (October 10, 1980), 28.

9. Ronald J. Sider, "Evangelism or Social Justice: Eliminating the Options," *Christianity Today* (October 8, 1976), 28, 29.

10. Ibid.

11. Charles C. Ryrie, "Perspectives on Social Ethics, Part III," *Bibliotheca Sacra* (July—September 1977), 215.

12. Ibid., p. 216.

13. Ibid., p. 227.

14. Ernest Pickering, "Our Social Responsibilities," *Vital Issues of the Hour*, No. 2, *Adult Instructor* (Schaumburg, IL: Regular Baptist Press, 1976), p. 24.

15. Henry, "Martyn Lloyd-Jones," p. 34.

9

The Individuals of the Church

We have already established that only regenerated individuals can Scripturally organize a church. The collective efforts of the members of the church are directed by the New Testament toward *care* for its own people and for a *witness* to the outside, unsaved world. The apostle Paul instructed, "Walk in wisdom toward them that are without, redeeming the time. Let your speech be alway with grace, seasoned with salt, that ye may know how ye ought to answer every man" (Col. 4:6, 7).

Dr. Ryrie shares a most vital distinction noted in the New Testament record concerning believers living in a wicked world and their conflict with it. He states: "Methods of effecting social change begin with the individual living up to his Christian responsibility, then involving the church in some instances in cooperative action, but never the church using the ruling political powers to bring about desired goals."[1]

Whereas the believer's limits in serving as a *church member* are clearly defined, he must realize he is also a *citizen* of society. This dual responsibility is certainly secondary, but yet a very real one. As a *citizen* the Christian must be concerned about his loyalty, his taxes, his involvement in the community, nation and world.

New evangelicals often point out how religious men have instigated and organized reforms. While this is a fact, it is also true that most of these did it not as leaders of churches or church organizations, but as individuals. One prime example commonly

cited is William Wilberforce, a disciple of John Wesley, who success-
fully attacked the evil slave trade business in England. In 1807 the
African slave trade by English merchants was abolished. What most
people do not realize was that Wilberforce was a member of the
English parliament. He was a great Christian leader and dedicated
crusader.[2]

In the review of J. Edwin Orr's book, *Revival and Social Changes*,
John Witmer notes that evangelicals have long been concerned
about social problems. Orr is quoted, "It is a popular fallacy that
Evangelical Christians have lacked a social conscience. In the perspective of history they have rendered notable service to humanity."[3]

In the review of Earl E. Cairn's book, *Saints and Society*, the
reviewer observes this significant conclusion:

> His thesis is that the reforms [slavery, prison, child labor,
> insane care, etc.] were accomplished by Christian indi-
> viduals, born again through faith in Christ as a result of
> the evangelical revivals under the Wesleys, Whitefield, and
> the evangelicals in the Church of England. The accom-
> plishment was not by the church directly, but by the indi-
> viduals who had been won to faith and action by the
> church.[4]

Some of the greatest reforms came from the influence of evan-
gelists and pastors, but these were individuals and often they were
not Scripturally correct. One of the most known abuses of religious
power was the American prohibition law passed in the early part
of the twentieth century. Prohibition was a dismal failure. Laws
might try to take alcoholic drinking away from the sinner, but not
until regeneration changes the sinner will he reform. Other so-
called "blue laws" were the ill-conceived attempt to force an unsaved
society to be motivated toward spiritual goals.

One of the most erratic, doctrinally incorrect crusaders was
Charles Finney in the nineteenth century. Nash states, "Although
Finney did not consistently support the widespread American
reform movement of the 1830s through the 1850s which his ministry had helped to launch, yet he joined social education to evangelism as no other major American has done."[5]

Another misguided evangelist is Billy Graham, who has wedded the social gospel to his evangelism. His decline from Biblical methodology and message to the near social gospel of ecumenical evangelism has hurt the cause of Christ immensely. He even testified in Washington in 1967 in favor of the socialistic Great Society poverty program.[6]

We also need to consider the growing influence of Jerry Falwell. Obviously a talented organizer and motivator, his exposure on national television and through the Moral Majority makes his views significant.

While Dr. Falwell claims to be a fundamentalist and a separatist, he seems to repudiate the traditional position of fundamentalism.

> However, we are not without our weakness [as Fundamentalists]. We tend to be negative and pessimistic. For too many years now, we have been sitting back waiting for apostasy to take over at any moment, and have nearly let the country go down the drain. We have been irresponsible as Christian citizens. We have almost totally avoided the political process and the social life of our country. We have neglected reaching the whole person for the cause of Christ. We have blasted the Liberals and derided the Evangelicals [i.e., new evangelicals] for their feeble attempts at the social application of the Gospel, while doing almost nothing ourselves.[7]

I cannot speak for all fundamentalists, but I do not believe that Jerry Falwell's indictment is a true representation of Regular Baptists. While there are extremists within the ranks of Regular Baptists, these few do not speak for the Association nor its churches and agencies. Regular Baptists as a whole are godly, separated, obedient Bible-believers. They are not negative—except where the Bible so commands; nor do they stress the coming apostasy—except to issue Biblical warning. Regular Baptists have not neglected their nation as indicated by more than sixty dedicated chaplains serving in the military. Many Association resolutions have urged patriotism, and countless prayers have been offered for the nation's leaders. Many godly lawmen serve in elected and appointed government offices. Others serve on school boards and in community and union organizations. Firemen, policemen, teachers and other government workers are common vocations. Regular Baptists have an active social ministry with four nationally approved social agencies plus other state approved agencies. These efforts may seem minimal compared to the enormous missionary outreach and building programs of our churches, but they are certainly not "almost nothing."

In Falwell's book *The Fundamentalist Phenomenon* he pleads for new evangelicals to work with his kind of fundamentalism to "turn America back to God."[8] He concludes, "We conservative Fundamentalists and Evangelicals [i.e., new evangelicals] can be used of God to bring about a great revival of true Christianity in America and the world in our lifetime."[9]

The fundamentalism of Jerry Falwell is *not* the fundamentalism of historical fundamentalism or of Regular Baptists. Sincere followers of this magnetic leader need to realize this, for they are being led by a new kind of fundamentalist who may not be one at all.

Individual Christian responsibility does extend to his world. But he does not reform society through his church ministry. The Great Commission is a *spiritual* mandate (Matt. 28:18–20). Still, he has a civic responsibility to support secular civil leaders, to defend one's country, to pay taxes, to vote, to work with unregenerate neighbors in society. He has social responsibilities as well, but they are limited. The needs of society (e.g., hunger and poverty) can be met through governmental programs which the Christian citizen supports by taxes and elected officials. (These benevolent programs exist because the United States was built on Biblical ethics and Christian compassion. Thus government has assumed many of the social responsibilities which Israel practiced.) Many Christians serve effectively in governmental or charitable organizations.

Donn Ketcham makes this interesting and noteworthy comment:

> It seems, then, that the responsibility for meeting the societal needs of man is *not* the responsibility of the *church.* Members of the church share this responsibility with the rest of mankind because they are a part of mankind but not because they are a part of the church.[10]

Notes:

1. Charles C. Ryrie, "Perspectives on Social Ethics, Part IV," *Bibliotheca Sacra* (October—December 1977), 327.

2. "The Age of Experiment and Reform," *Eerdman's Handbook to Christianity in America* (Grand Rapids: Wm. B. Eerdmans, 1983), p. 189.

3. John A. Witmer, "Periodical Reviews," *Bibliotheca Sacra* (October—December 1974), 359.

4. C. A. Nash, "Book Review," *Bibliotheca Sacra* (January—March 1961), 81.

5. Lee Nash, "Evangelism and Social Concern," p. 139.

6. Ibid., p. 145.

7. Jerry Falwell, *The Fundamentalist Phenomenon* (Garden City, NY: Doubleday Co., 1981), p. 220.

8. Ibid., p. 222.

9. Ibid., p. 223.

10. Ketcham, *The World Hurts!* p. 40.

IV

Review of
Social
Issues

"As we have, therefore, opportunity, let us do good unto all men, especially unto them who are of the household of faith" (Galatians 6:10).

10

Abortion: The Murder of Society

America is becoming a land drenched in blood! Every year since 1973, over one million innocent, helpless infants have been murdered! With no legal recourse to protect them and practically no medical personnel to defend them against brutal, deliberate death, the unborn of the most affluent, sophisticated nation in the world face destruction.

On January 22, 1973, the United States Supreme Court (*Roe v. Wade*) decided the unborn have no right to life if their mothers choose to terminate life by the twenty-fourth week of pregnancy. (A medical doctor's consent is needed after this.) Abortion is the second most-common surgical procedure today. It is estimated that ten million babies have been murdered since 1973. One estimate put it at sixteen million.[1] Thirty percent of all pregnancies are terminated by legal abortion. One-third of the women are teenagers; three-fourths are unmarried women.

We have laws to protect children from abuse and women from rapists but none to protect the unborn! In the Los Angeles area, the lifeless, mutilated bodies of 500 unborn children were discovered in a massive trash container. It had been rented by a medical lab which had gone out of business. These bodies were variously developed; some were four pounds or more. The Los Angeles officials discovered 400 more bodies at the owner's home. After more investigation by the coroner's office, the final count was over 17,000! All of this murder is legal.[2]

The moral issue of abortion goes beyond the mother who murders her own infant and beyond the judges who have given legal sanction to this infanticide (killing of infants). The responsibility lies at the feet of the medical profession. How can the vast majority of physicians and hospital personnel condone and even profit from this wickedness? The Surgeon General of the United States, Dr. C. Everett Koop, comments:

> Certainly, we have come to an age where the Hippocratic tradition of preserving human life means little. One could say without hesitation that we are at the crossroads of the corruption of medicine with the corruption of law. Corruption of law came first in this country with the U.S. Supreme Court abortion decision of 1973. The corruption of medicine followed.[3]

For physicians to treat an unwanted pregnancy as a disease boggles the mind! One medical doctor expressed it this way:

> Physicians are not sociologists, nor theologians, nor economists. We do not judge the quality of life, we are simply healers. Unwarranted pregnancy may be, indeed, a social problem, but it is not an illness. If we, as physicians, are to treat social or other non-medical problems, our patients will not be too long in realizing that we have abandoned the ancient and sacred role of "healer."[4]

Abortion on demand is a means of infanticide. Pharaoh in ancient Egypt practiced it (Exod. 1:16). Herod practiced it in Bethlehem (Matt. 2:16–18). The ancient Romans practiced it in a brutal way by allowing parents to abandon unwanted children on the outskirts of Rome to die from animals or exposure. Often unscrupulous merchants would rescue these children and raise them as slaves or prostitutes. Sometimes Christians would rescue the children, but this was scandalous to the Roman authorities because it shamed them.

This generation is fast becoming perverted in its value of human life. The unborn infant is a "fetus" or a "P.O.C." (product of conception), not a person. Why did this brutal, heartless attitude originate?

The major reason is because this generation is the product of the humanistic philosophy taught in the public schools and the absence of spiritual values which should have resulted from Biblical teaching. Man is an animal according to evolutionary theory, and thus morality is relative, not absolute as based on God and His laws. This "new morality" has been called "situation ethics." The idea that "the end justifies the means" permits people to sin without fear.

The careless, amoral community life in the ghettos in many inner cities defies normal social solutions. Poverty, blackmail, illicit drugs and prostitution cheapen life, causing unborn children to be problems not blessings. Abortion seems to be a logical solution. But abortion afflicts all of society, not just the ghettos.

Fundamentalists ought to know what the Bible teaches on abortion. Since there is no direct command against abortion, the following points should be considered:

1. Children are the gift of God: Genesis 33:5; Psalms 113:9; 127:3.

2. Conception is God's design: Genesis 1:28; 29:33; 30:22; Ruth 4:5, 13; 1 Samuel 1:19, 20.

3. The prenatal infant is considered a life: Psalms 51:5; 139:13, 14; Isaiah 49:1; Jeremiah 1:5; Luke 1:41, 44.

4. Destruction or harm to prenatal life was penalized under the Mosaic Law: Exodus 21:22-25.

5. There is a difference between birth control which prevents conception (no life) and abortion which destroys life.

Let's look more closely at the question, *When* does human life begin? Dr. Daniel R. Hinthorn, assistant professor of medicine, University of Kansas, analyzes the issue with this comment:

> Life is certainly present after fertilization of the egg by the sperm when only one cell is present, but is this human life? . . . However the question of when God gives the fetus a soul, or when God looks upon an individual as a person, or when God inscribes a name in his book, is more difficult.[5]

One thing is certain: the new life in the womb is sacred to God and known to God. "Before I formed thee in the belly I knew thee; and before thou camest forth out of the womb I sanctified thee, and I ordained thee a prophet unto the nations" (Jer. 1:5). Genesis 25:23 states that God knew who was in the womb: "And the

LORD said unto her, Two nations are in thy womb, and two manner of people shall be separated from thy bowels; and the one people shall be stronger than the other people; and the elder shall serve the younger." Again, Isaiah 42:24 indicates God's involvement in the formation of the fetus: "Thus saith the LORD, thy redeemer, and he that formed thee from the womb, I am the LORD that maketh all things; that stretcheth forth the heavens alone; that spreadeth abroad the earth by myself."

But the most articulate passage is David's comments on his prenatal existence: "For thou hast possessed my reins: thou hast covered me in my mother's womb. I will praise thee; for I am fearfully and wonderfully made: marvellous are thy works; and that my soul knoweth right well. My substance was not hid from thee, when I was made in secret, and curiously wrought in the lowest parts of the earth" (Ps. 139:13-15). Then note the amazing truth of the eternal God's involvement and concern about the unborn child in Psalm 139:16 (NASB): "Thine eyes have seen my unformed substance; And in Thy book they were all written, The days that were ordained for me, When as yet there was not one of them."

The word for "substance" in the Hebrew is *golem*. It is only used here. It seems to mean rolled or folded together.[6] This suggests the time of implantation of the embryo in the wall of the uterus, which is approximately seven to eight days after conception.[7] This gives unique insight into the life of the fetus and the fact that it may well be a human person. Most fundamentalists agree that human life begins at conception; however, conception and birth contain so much mystery that no one can be dogmatic. But one thing is certain: God treasures the unborn in the womb and even records the unborn child.

The issue, then, is not really whether a woman has the right to do with her own body as she sees fit, but that she is given the right to destroy a life of another individual as she pleases. Dr. Koop states:

> By the time a baby is 18 to 25 days old, long before the mother is sure she is pregnant, the heart is already beating. At 45 days after conception, you can pick up the electro-encephalgraphic (sic) waves from the baby's developing brain. At 8 weeks, there is not only a brain, but fingerprints

on the hands have already formed and except for the size, will never change. By the 9th and 10th weeks, the thyroid and adrenal glands are functioning. The baby can squint, swallow, move his tongue and the sex hormones are already present. By 12 and 13 weeks, he has fingernails, he sucks his thumb and can recoil from pain. In the 4th month the growing baby is 8 to 10 inches in height. In the 5th month there is a time of lengthening and strengthening of the developing infant. Skin, hair and nails grow. Sweat glands arise. Oil glands excrete. This is the month in which the movements of the baby are felt by his mother. In the 6th month the baby responds to light and sound. He can sleep and awake. He gets hiccups and can hear the beat of his mother's heart. Survival outside the womb is now possible.[8]

What about therapeutic abortions for medical or criminal reasons? Pregnancies which are caused by incest or rape or which endanger the life of the mother are different in perspective than "abortion on demand." Most of these peculiar situations do not require abortion as a viable solution, and they comprise less than 5 percent of all abortions.[9] In these cases abortion may only compound the problem and bring even greater mental anguish. Decisions which involve such personal matters ought to be left to the responsible family members with counsel from their pastor and a competent physician.

When a deformed infant in the womb is discovered, the world's solution is abortion. But many testimonies abound that accepting such a child often becomes a blessing to the family when it is accepted in the light of Scripture (e.g., Rom. 8:28). Anna Marie Dahlquist, who was faced with this situation, states:

> What would it be like to raise a mongoloid child? I knew three Christian couples with Down's syndrome babies. I thought about how, without exception, they had stated, "This child has been a blessing to our family." In each case they had said, the family had been drawn closer together, and the older children had learned gentleness and patience through the relationship.[10]

Another fallacious argument is that abortions save the lives of many mothers. Dr. Christopher Tietze, head of abortion research at the Population Council (financed by the Rockefeller Foundation) believes that 1,500 pregnancy related deaths have been averted because of legal abortions.[11] Such nonsense! To sacrifice at least 10,000,000 lives to save perhaps 1,500 mothers (and this number is only conjecture) is strange mathematics indeed!

While fundamentalists do not claim to have all the answers, they can categorically declare abortion on demand is NOT the answer. Until judges, social workers, medical doctors, hospital administrators and politicians recognize the immorality of this murder of helpless persons, the massacre of infants will continue. The emotional guilt and physical repercussions alone should rule out abortion as a viable solution. But when the eternal judgment of almighty God is considered, every murderer ought to tremble.

Fundamentalists ought to investigate judges' and politicians' views on abortion before they vote. When fundamentalists join social or political organizations, they should be careful not to become identified with an alien religious movement. Pro-life groups may well be Roman Catholic social organizations which want broader membership for public relations reasons.

Fundamentalists must warn society of this insane destruction of its next generation. It is a national crisis. Perhaps only a Constitutional Convention to amend the Constitution will reduce the slaughter of innocent and helpless infants.

Notes:

1. "Expert Says 1,500 Saved by Abortions," *Houston Chronicle* (March 8, 1984).

2. Mark Gladstone, "Evidence Sought in Deaths of Fetuses," *Los Angeles Times* (February 7, 1982).

3. C. Everett Koop, "Abortion and the Future," *Abortion in America* (Elyria, OH: Intercessors for America, 1980), p. 7.

4. Dan Lyons and Billy James Hargis, *Thou Shalt Not Kill . . . My Babies* (Tulsa: Christian Crusade Publications, 1977), p. 44.

5. Daniel R. Hinthorn, "When Does Human Life Begin?" *Christianity Today* (March 24, 1978), 36.

6. Ibid.

7. Ibid.

8. Mark Elam, "In Defense of Life," *The Christian Alternative* (March 1982), 2.

9. Anna Marie Dahlquist, "Then You Can Have an Abortion," *Eternity* (March 1981), 42.

10. Ibid.

11. *Houston Chronicle* (March 8, 1984).

11

Alcoholism:
The Curse
of Society

America faces an internal cancer of which most citizens and many Christians are not really aware. Alcoholism causes tragedy of such magnitude it cannot be realistically measured. More than 250,000 people have been killed in the past ten years in auto accidents related to alcohol use. It is estimated that only 1 in 200 drunk drivers is apprehended by the police. One in every 10 drivers on Friday or Saturday night is drunk![1]

Teenagers consume enormous quantities of alcohol. Thirty-one percent of all high schoolers are regular drinkers, and an estimated three million fourteen- to seventeen-year-olds are problem drinkers. Add to this eleven million American adults who are problem drinkers, and you begin to see the scope of the problem. Then consider that one in twenty children lives with a parent who is an alcoholic. Think of the suffering and fear in these homes. These children, of course, are more likely to become alcoholics themselves.

The United States Department of Health and Human Services gives these astounding statistics:

> Alcohol causes or contributes to one-half of all auto accidents. Alcohol is involved in 50% of rape perpetrators, 72% of assaults, 72% of robberies, 18,000 deaths and 10 million job injuries or job accidents, 83% of fire and burn victims, 69% of drowning victims, 64% of suicide attempts, and 10,000 suicide deaths.[2]

More recent studies indicate these statistics should be increased. Alcoholism's terrible influence is on the rise!

One of the most frightening revelations on alcoholism is its horrible effects on the unborn. Dr. Ian Holzman, physician with the Department of Pediatrics, Pittsburgh School of Medicine, states, "Alcoholism, when ingested in excess during pregnancy, results in problems for the developing fetus."[3] Some of the abnormalities include small size, altered features, heart and spine defects, mental retardation, behavior problems and poor growth; these are the most obvious. The ancient Greeks and Hebrews forbade alcoholic consumption by women trying to conceive. But today's liberated women "have come a long way, baby." Irresponsibility, immorality and indulgence characterize many worldly mothers-to-be.

Consider also the politicians who lowered the drinking age from twenty-one to eighteen or nineteen. They must face the moral and eternal consequences of their action. Bill Stokes in his article "Drinking Age Should Be Uniform" observes:

> We follow the lead of the alcohol-beverage industry like lobotomized sheep. There is so much money involved that we get bought without even realizing we were for sale. . . . We seem incapable of dealing with the situation in any rational manner. There can be no other explanation for the way the nation is sliced up into state-size drinking areas: 21 in Illinois, 18 in Wisconsin, 19 in Iowa, 20 in Nebraska.[4]

As recently as 1977 the federal government spent twice as much on dental research as it did on alcoholism research.[5] If that does not upset the mind, this next statement will. The American Medical Association twenty-five years ago astounded society with the declaration that alcoholism is a *disease!* Not a sin, not a moral weakness, but a disease named Jellinek's Disease. Rather than considering it shameful or wicked, the AMA made alcoholism a consequence of society. Such nonsense baffles thinking people. It is the only "disease" which is contracted by an act of the will (one decides to start drinking) and the only disease that is caused by neither germ nor virus.

Alcoholism has similarities with a disease in that once the social drinker becomes dependent on alcohol, he can be treated and cured.

But unless the alcoholic recognizes his own responsibility and wills himself to get help, there is no real help. Usually a drinker does not wish to change; he must be confronted with his hopelessness. Vernon E. Johnson bluntly states:

> Alcoholism is a fatal disease, 100% fatal. Nobody survives alcoholism that remains unchecked. We would estimate that 10 percent of the drinkers in America will become alcoholic, and that these people will not be able to stop drinking by themselves. It is a myth that alcoholics have some spontaneous insight and then seek treatment.[6]

Why do people begin a habit which will claim 10 percent addiction? (Some authorities claim one in five drinkers will become alcoholic.) The major reason for alcoholism, according to Dr. George Vaillant, who has made a long-time study and written *The Natural History of Alcoholism: Causes, Patterns, and Paths to Recovery*, is peer pressure. He says that the "alcoholic personality" is a result, not the cause, of alcoholism. It is not caused by genetic reasons, although the tendency to drink is passed on in the family.[7]

Dr. Vaillant concludes some ethnic groups are more susceptible to alcoholism, such as the Irish, who are seven times more frequently alcoholic than Italians. He also concludes there are no biological causes. He diagnoses an alcoholic as a person who discovers he is doing things when drinking that he regrets afterward.[8]

Recognizing the several phases of alcoholism will help Christians know how to reach and assist alcoholics. The pre-alcoholic phase occurs when the social or casual drinker crosses a mystical line into the uncontrollable and dependent stage. A change of drinking habits then occurs. Alcohol becomes necessary for "euphoria." Tension is released and a state of personal contentment is temporarily reached. Blackouts or amnesia will begin to occur occasionally during drinking bouts. More and more alcohol is required to help the drinker "cope." Sneaking drinks and hiding bottles is common.

Next is the crucial phase characterized by lying, manipulation of people, excuses, lack of interest in family and religious matters. The drinker drinks alone, consuming increasing quantities, as he becomes more and more antisocial.

Finally, the alcoholic moves into the <u>chronic phase</u> with periods of uncontrollable, compulsive drinking, often for days or weeks. No sense of responsibility or guilt restrains him. Utter disregard for family, job and even food and shelter brings physical deterioration. The "shakes," along with nauseated, dehydrated suffering, bring the drinker near death. Liver and brain damage are rampant. Total defeat with eventual death or insanity is inevitable.[9]

One peculiar trait often found in alcoholics is the "dry-drunk syndrome." This occurs when the alcoholic is miserable even when NOT drinking. His antisocial manner is still present. It is intoxication without alcohol![10]

The major hindrance to recovering an alcoholic is his self-denial. He refuses to see or admit his condition of addiction. It usually requires a confrontation by his family or employers if he is ever to face the reality of alcoholism.

The record of success by modern psychiatry in aiding recovery is a national scandal. In fact, Dr. Vaillant, who is a Harvard psychiatrist himself, deplores the poor results of his profession. He notes that traditional psychiatric approaches may be helpful for treating accompanying symptoms, such as despair, paranoia or anxiety, but they are nearly useless in dealing with the underlying nature of alcoholism itself.[11] He further states,

> Psychiatrists have been trained that alcoholism is a problem which comes from early-childhood experiences, but aren't taught how to treat alcoholics. They go after those "underlying causes"; [but the] treatment doesn't work, the alcoholic gets worse and the psychiatrist decides that the disease is intractable.[12]

The only truly successful victory comes when Christ, Who has power to forgive and to change the heart, takes control. While some alcoholics have received Christ, experienced dramatic reversal and are never tempted again, this is not the normal experience. The average situation usually requires the alcoholic to sober up and dry out before spiritual results can be accomplished.

The wise Christian counselor will not hesitate to use varied means to reach the mind and heart of the alcoholic with the Word of God. Hospitalization, trained counselors and Alcoholics Anonymous can be used, especially in the first step of recovery. Often the alcoholic needs the testimonies and support of others who have "been there" and survived. Since the chemistry of the body has become dependent upon the drug, a great deal of patience and forbearance is needed. One study reports that drinkers who abstain for a year have a fair opportunity for success.

Alcoholics Anonymous is criticized for its weakness and humanistic approach, but it has met the need for many recovered alcoholics. Furthermore, Al-Anon, Al-Ateen and Al-Atot give help and support to the families and friends of alcoholics. Some people might lament that the local church is sometimes bypassed, but the fact of the matter is that most local churches and pastors would not understand the alcoholic's mentality and chemical crises. Alcoholics Anonymous should never be substituted for the church, but it can supplement the local church. Most recovered alcoholics, even Christians, need the type of support that can only come from other recovered alcoholics.

The devastation from alcohol abuse takes a toll on every member of the family. Even children learn to cover up the disgrace and manipulate their friends and relatives. The following account is the testimony of a dear Christian woman whom this author has counseled over a period of five years. Her story can be multiplied many times over in scores of fundamental churches.

> I was saved as a youngster at the age of ten, but I really came to the assurance of my salvation years later.
>
> When I married my husband, he was already a problem drinker, experiencing personal and financial problems. Later, it was evident he had severe behavior problems, for he would lie, connive about money, write bad checks, hide mail, neglect paying bills, etc. Conditions continued to worsen over the years, and I turned to God for deliverance.
>
> Since I wanted to be a faithful, compatible and obedient wife, I permitted his overbearing and unacceptable behavior, showering him with love and affection in an attempt to try and win him to Christ. His abuse and neglect of the children and me was tolerated because I felt God would honor this submission.
>
> Alcoholism is a progressive disease, and after years of heartache and oppression, without realizing it, I had become

emotionally conditioned to react to his behavior. I was a "co-alcoholic" or "co-dependent." In other words, he was dependent on alcohol and I was dependent on him. My whole life revolved around his behavior and the problems it was causing. I tried to find solutions so we could live peacefully as a family. *This describes the dynamics of the disease of alcoholism in action.*

You have a person whose actions demand the center of attention. When a person is having problems, it's human nature (and God's desire) to want to try and find a solution to "fix" the problems so the person will be happy again, because the sooner they are happy, the sooner everyone else will be happy. So everyone flutters around, trying to "fix" this person's problems. The sad reality is that in alcoholism the problems are only symptoms of what is really wrong. The root of the problem is alcohol, and as long as the alcohol is present, the problems will never go away. They will worsen as the disease progresses. Only when the alcohol is removed or the people affected by someone who uses it get into a recovery program can the tendency to be drawn into the disease be dealt with.

As I was unaware of this at the time, I was victimized by the disease and became as sick as he was! Maybe worse, for I had discounted my true feelings and compromised my value system to the point that I became a casualty—confused, frightened, angry and severely depressed. My self-esteem and self-confidence were totally undermined. I felt guilty when I ever considered my own happiness instead of trying to make him happy. Now I know that true happiness comes from within.

You see, it's a family disease. The family suffers as much or more than the alcoholic. As the alcoholic drinks to avoid dealing with life's issues, they are—in a sense—anesthetized against their feelings. Because they are unable to look at their own shortcomings and manage their lives, they blame their problems mainly on those they live with and work with. The family gets the brunt of their emotions.

Our children were also victims, and our daughter (now married) suffered greatly because she played the hero. She always was striving to please her father, but, of course, he never approved of her numerous accomplishments. (He didn't have the capacity to do so while drinking.) Instead of approval, she was many times criticized and would avoid him. Our son withdrew and was disappointed on numerous occasions whenever his father failed to do what he said he would do. (He didn't have the capacity to keep his promises.)

Church, school and other activities often became a shelter away from the house—especially for the children, as they could escape the tension and pressure at home. Their needs for companionship, love and support were met by their friends. Our family life left much to be desired.

This pattern continued for perhaps ten years. I was confused and frustrated that I was not winning my husband to Christ. Also, for me, the world's methods (Al-Anon, Alcoholics Anonymous and therapy) seemed to conflict with God's. I became more angry and frustrated, longing for relief and not seeing it anywhere.

Finally, my doctor was insistent I get help; so I contacted my pastor. We visited an alcoholic counselor. I started opening myself up to the information available to enlighten me in my circumstances, and relief started to come. Eventually my eyes opened to the reality of the alcoholic dilemma. I could finally understand that he could not help his condition and that my actions, no matter how noble, would not reach him. I learned that all alcoholics cry for help, and I knew I was unable to hear those cries.

With professional guidance, all of the family and a real good friend met with my husband to present the reality of how his behavior while drinking affected each of us. There was an *intervention*, presenting reality in a loving, caring way so he could hear our cries for him to seek help— cries made in such a way as to penetrate all those many defenses he was hiding behind.

Much anger, threats of violence, tears and prayers led up to this crisis in which he must face the fact he was near death. A drinking alcoholic is so deluded, he cannot know reality. Intervention is designed to present reality to alcoholics and gives them an opportunity to know they are sick and in need of help.

At first my husband refused, but he finally met with us as a family. Since he was reluctant to get help, I told him that if he wanted to continue drinking, I was through with him. I said we would give him the rest of our lives if he would give us thirty days in a recovery program. At our son's urging, he agreed to go to a chemical dependency unit. When I visited him a week later, his whole attitude had changed; he was glad he had decided to go. He had been detoxified and watched carefully after admission; he was in the process of being restored as a human being.

He could now see the heartache alcohol addiction had caused himself as well as his family. It's so tragic, so sad—the many, many losses suffered and the wasted years of productive living, enslaved to a chemical; desperate, sick; not knowing how to get free; afraid to live and afraid to die.

Alcoholism affects a person physically, mentally, spiritually and psychologically; and the longer it's allowed to go unchallenged, the less chance a person has of being restored to a total, healthy person. My husband is now a responsible, caring human being and can make choices for his own benefit. I hope and pray he will choose Christ as his Savior.

I am continuing in a recovery program so I can heal my wounds. It's not enough to know and understand the facts about your situation. As I said before, I had been conditioned to react in a co-alcoholic manner. My recovery is dependent on breaking that old conditioning so I also can be restored to a total, healthy, responsible, caring human being. Those patterns have to be addressed and dealt with, or they will continue. Al-Anon has helped immensely, as well as getting some counseling on the disease of alcoholism and its affect on my behavior.

The redeeming factor of all the pain and loss associated with living in active alcoholism is the spiritual awakening realized by no longer giving lip service to faith in God but coming to a total dependence on God, experiencing Him in a real sense. Without having gone through it, I dare say I would have missed the opportunity to grow and mature as a person, spiritually and otherwise.

All situations are different. The ideal is for all parties to be in a recovery program together. Sometimes this isn't how it works out, but a recovery program *is* necessary to break the symptoms or patterns I've described. Without help, you are continually drawn back into the alcoholic system.

It's paramount to be aware of the circumstances with individuals or in families where chemical abuse is present; and in order to be of help, you should learn the facts about chemical dependency. Alcoholism, drug abuse and chemical dependency are all the same thing. It's a family disease where perfectly healthy people wind up very frightened, confused, frustrated, isolated, angry and depressed while they are doing their dead level best to be the best they know how to be.

What does Scripture teach about alcoholism? The classic book which researches the use of wine in the Scriptures is *Bible Wines or Laws of Fermentation and Wines of the Ancients* by William Patton. This book was published in 1871 by Dr. Patton, who wished to confront the wicked habits of New York City where he was a pastor. He began his crusade against social drinking with a message on Romans 12:2 on the "Sabbath evening of September 17, 1820." Dr. Patton said, "Whilst the drunkard is a guilty person, the retail seller is more guilty, the wholesale dealer still more guilty, and the distiller who converts the staff of life, the benevolent gift of God, into the arrows of death, is the most guilty."[14]

His conclusion that there are two kinds of wine, alcoholic and nonalcoholic, has been substantiated by language scholars. Jack Van Impe summarizes Patton's research as follows: (1) The Hebrew words translated "wine" in the Bible do not always mean fermented or intoxicating wine; (2) the Hebrew word *yayin*, most often translated "wine" in the Old Testament, means grape juice in any form—fermented or unfermented. The true meaning can only be determined by the text; (3) the Hebrew word *tirosh*, also translated "wine" in all but one possible case, means "new wine," "unfermented wine." This word was used repeatedly in the original text in the places where wine has a good textural connotation; (4) many wines of the ancients were boiled or filtered to prevent fermentation, and these were often considered the best wines.[15]

So then the context where the word for wine is used determines how it should be interpreted. Van Impe quotes Ewing with his excellent explanation:

> . . . If a reader will just consider the context surrounding the word he can easily understand whether the fermented or unfermented grape juice was intended. Wherever the use of wine is prohibited or discouraged, it means the fermented

wine. Where its use is encouraged and is spoken of as something for our good it means the unfermented.[16]

Robert Teachout, Hebrew scholar, who wrote his doctoral thesis on this subject at Dallas Theological Seminary, would agree with this principle that the context determines the meaning.[17]

The finest treatment of the subject in the Bible in the light of history, Scripture and the present-day culture is the brief but excellent booklet by Kenneth Brown, *The Use of Wine in the Bible*. A wealth of material on all the words used in the Old and New Testaments, along with the customs of various cultures, makes this booklet indispensable. For example, distilled alcohol was not discovered until after Bible times; thus, the fermented wine was very low in alcoholic content, not exceeding 15 percent. Another interesting, but revolting, bit of information is how the Roman Catholic church and many liberal church organizations have approved the production and use of liquor. Some of Dr. Brown's conclusions are as follows:

> The general terms for the fruit of the vine (*yayin* and *oinos*) do not correspond to the English word for the beverage called "wine." These Biblical terms mean the fruit of the vine without reference to the presence or absence of alcohol. . . .
>
> In all ages men have recognized the distinction between fresh juice of the vine and that which is fermented and produces intoxication. God has sanctioned and blessed the former and condemned and judged the latter. Every attempt to bring divine approval upon beverages which God has condemned in His Word is doomed to failure. Amen and so be it![18]

Many Scripture passages prohibit drinking alcoholic wine. For example Proverbs 23:31, "Look [Hebrew: to lust, desire] not thou upon the wine when it is red, when it giveth his colour in the cup, when it moveth itself aright." Again, Proverbs 20:1 states, "Wine is a mocker, strong drink is raging: and whosoever is deceived thereby is not wise."

The only wise and obedient solution is *total abstinence*. The control of the Holy Spirit is contrasted with the power of alcohol (Eph. 5:18).

Surely the two are diametrically opposed. The habitual drunkard is warned that he cannot expect eternal life (1 Cor. 6:10). But the passage that nails the coffin for social drinking is Galatians 5:21 where the word "drunkenness" *(methais)* should be translated "drinkings" or "occasions of drinking." It is not necessarily over consumption, as used in 1 Peter 4:3 and 1 Corinthians 5:11 *(methusos)*, but *drinking itself* that is a work of the flesh (Rom. 13:13, 14). No believer can justify social drinking or casual drinking because his body is the temple of God (1 Cor. 6:19). Paul Tassell rings the bell with, "Holiness and highballs are not harmonious. Christ and cocktails are not compatible."[19] Furthermore, one's drinking can cause another believer to stumble (1 Cor. 8:9). Pastors and deacons are strictly forbidden to drink (1 Tim. 3:3, 8).

A local church can have several ministries for alcoholics. The pastor should realize that he needs special training to have an effective ministry. He should research the subject and attend some area seminars. The leaders of such seminars may not understand the Biblical teaching on sin, but they do have knowledge of the chemical and medical aspects of alcoholism. The family members of an alcoholic desperately need counsel and support. The strength and love of God are powerful allies (Gal. 6:2). The church is limited if it does not comprehend the spiritual, social and emotional trials of the family in stress. Information should be given to church members for, no doubt, many have friends or relatives who are afflicted. The dangers of teenage drinking should be stressed.

To help the alcoholic is a very difficult challenge. A treatment which has been quite successful is called INTERVENTION. The originator of the program, Vernon E. Johnson, has written a book explaining it, *I'll Quit Tomorrow.*

The Christian citizen can do at least three things: (1) support civil officials who stand against the social trends and influence of the liquor industry; (2) protest liquor advertising; (3) refrain from purchasing commodities produced by firms which are owned by the liquor industry.

Make no pretense about the issue of social drinking! It is destroying society many times faster than high taxes or communism. The Hollywood film producers make drinking look glamorous, but the warning against it must be sounded. It must be named what it really is: *moral sin.*

In 1978 the General Association of Regular Baptist Churches passed a resolution condemning social drinking. A copy of this fine exposé can be obtained from the GARBC, Post Office Box 95500, Schaumburg, Illinois 60195. It urges total abstinence from alcoholic beverages, citing logical and Scriptural reasons.

One final question, Why do new evangelicals, whose declared passion is to correct social injustice, not fight *this* social battle? Why do they not criticize the liquor industry and warn of its evils? John Witmer makes this point in his review of a wishy-washy article on wine drinking customs in New Testament times. He comments:

> An anomaly of today is the mushrooming social problem of alcohol abuse in the face of declining opposition to drinking alcoholic beverages among evangelical Christians, especially those who insist that the church must relate to social issues. It has always puzzled this reviewer why those in the forefront of social involvement and concern—both liberal and evangelical—have had little to say about the liquor industry and its tragic social results.[20]

Dr. Witmer concludes his review with this excellent evaluation of the Bible record: "The practice of wine-drinking in biblical times gives little support for the advocates of moderation today, especially in the light of the contemporary abuse of alcohol. For the Christian, abstinence is still the best witness."[21]

Several books are available for research to help alcoholics and their families. An extensive bibliography is given on pages 00-00. Fundamentalists must face this growing menace which threatens the life and safety of the people of the nation.

Notes:

1. Candy Lightner, M.A.D.D. 1983, p. 3.
2. Claudine Henderson, Houston Regional Council on Alcoholism, n.d.
3. M. McDevitt Rubin, "Taboo on Alcohol during Pregnancy Goes Way Back," *The Pittsburgh Press* (September 21, 1983).
4. Bill Stokes, "Drinking Age Should Be Uniform," *Houston Post* (October 17, 1983).

5. Kathleen Whalen Fitzgerald, "Living with Jellinek's Disease," *Newsweek* (October 17, 1983), 22.

6. Vernon E. Johnson, *I'll Quit Tomorrow* (New York: Harper & Row, 1973), p. 1.

7. Jane O'Reilly, "New Insights into Alcoholism," *Time* (April 25, 1983), 88.

8. Ibid.

9. "Symptoms of Alcoholism," Austin, TX: Texas Commission on Alcoholism.

10. R. J. Solberg, *The Dry-Drunk Syndrome* (Center City, MN: Hazelden, 1980), p. 3.

11. O'Reilly, p. 89.

12. Ibid.

13. Barbara R. Thompson, "Alcoholism: Even the Church Is Hurting," *Christianity Today* (August 5, 1983), 28.

14. William Patton, *Bible Wines or Laws of Fermentation and Wines of the Ancients* (Oklahoma City: Sane Press, n.d.), p. 10.

15. Jack Van Impe, *Alcohol: The Beloved Enemy* (Nashville: Thomas Nelson, 1980), p. 111.

16. Ibid., p. 118.

17. Ibid., p. 115.

18. Kenneth I. Brown, *The Use of Wine in the Bible*, pp. 23, 24.

19. Paul Tassell, "Three Reasons Why a Christian Should Not Be a Social Drinker," p. 4.

20. John Witmer, "Book Review," *Bibliotheca Sacra* (October—December 1975) 359.

21. Ibid.

12

Crime:
The Violence
in Society

The crime rate is increasing faster than the population; the judicial system in America is coddling criminals and restricting law enforcers; the prognosis for the future looks bleak. The fundamentalist should seek some answers. The insight into this social nightmare is the Scriptures.

> This know also, that in the last days perilous times shall come.
>
> For men shall be lovers of their own selves, covetous, boasters, proud, blasphemers, disobedient to parents, unthankful, unholy,
>
> Without natural affection, trucebreakers, false accusers, incontinent, fierce, despisers of those that are good,
>
> Traitors, heady, highminded, lovers of pleasures more than lovers of God;
>
> Having a form of godliness, but denying the power thereof: from such turn away.
>
> For of this sort are they which creep into houses, and lead captive silly women laden with sins, led away with divers lusts,
>
> Ever learning, and never able to come to the knowledge of the truth (2 Tim. 3:1-7).

Jesus taught that in the end of this age, "iniquity shall abound" (Matt. 24:12). "Iniquity" literally means "lawlessness" or the rejection of authority. John wrote that sin is lawlessness (1 John 3:4: "sin is the transgression of the law"). Sin is the real cause of violence and crime.

God in His wisdom established the human means to deal with crime. The foundation of this method is the ultimate punishment, capital punishment. This could be defined as the "death penalty for crime." The Lord instructed Noah following the Deluge to establish certain rules for mankind; one of these was capital punishment (Gen. 9:6).

The attack on capital punishment usually comes from those in society who disregard the Scriptures as authoritative. The misguided arguments against capital punishment center on humanitarian reasons and an appeal to the love of God. More concern is shown for the criminal who has violated the most sacred trust, human life, than for the victim and his family.

Noah was not the only one to receive instructions regarding capital punishment. The Mosaic law established capital punishment for the crime of murder (Exod. 21:12; Num. 35:16–31); for working on the Sabbath (Exod. 35:2); for cursing parents (Lev. 20:9); for adultery (Lev. 20:10); for incest (Lev. 20:11–13); for sodomy (Lev. 20:15, 16); for false prophesying (Deut. 13:1–10; 18:20); for idolatry (Deut. 17:2–7); for incorrigible juvenile delinquency (Deut. 21:18–23); for rape (Deut. 22:25); for keeping a dangerous beast (Exod. 21:29); for kidnapping (Exod. 21:16); for someone who intrudes into a sacred place (Num. 1:51; 3:10, 38; 18:7). Stoning was the usual method of execution.

Romans 13:1–7 supports the fact that capital punishment is valid for secular governments which are established by God and authorized to use the "sword." While some scholars try to negate the sword as condoning capital punishment, it seems quite obvious the sword is not used for manicures! Shedd and Godet, both respected commentators, teach that Paul was supporting the right of secular government to exercise capital punishment.[1]

Whether capital punishment is a realistic deterrent to major crime is not the issue. Many criminologists believe it certainly is. The moral and Biblical issue is that when one man takes the life (sheds blood or life "soul") then his "soul" or physical life must be taken by society (Gen. 9:6). True, many civilizations and cultures have abused it, but that does not change the issue. Even the Supreme Court of the United States has ruled that it is constitutional when proper trials and appeals have been followed.

An interesting idea has been proposed by Professor Samuel Levensohn of the University of Central Florida. He suggests that all murderers, rapists, etc., be put in exile on a South Sea island to live out their lives in banishment, a "forbidden community of men." Another innovative view by Graeme Newman, Dean of the School of Criminal Justice at the State University of New York at Albany, suggests that electric shocks and public flogging should take the place of imprisonment.

William Bellshaw sums up the matter this way:

> The force of God's Word compels the Christian to recognize God's authority in the matter of captial punishment. God will hold all responsible who flagrantly disregard His estimate of human life. The Bible does not countenance any view which attempts to shift this responsiblity for wrongdoing from the individual to society (Romans 14:12). Each person is accountable to God for his actions. In like manner, each believer is accountable to God for his attitude to the revelation God has given in His Word. This is the final authority for the child of God.[3]

One final thought: The Bible believer, while not belligerent, has every right to protect his home, family, life and possessions from potential violators. He should not seek revenge once violated, however; that is the responsibility of civil authority.

Notes:

1. Charles C. Ryrie, "The Doctrine of Capital Punishment," *Bibliotheca Sacra* (July—September 1972), 215.

2. Helen Gideon, "A Shocking Approach to Crime," *Houston Chronicle*, (March 4, 1984), citing Graeme Newman, *Just and Painful*.

3. William G. Bellshaw, "Capital Punishment—Crime or Command?" San Francisco Baptist Theological Seminary.

13

Divorce and Remarriage: The Breakdown of Society

The purpose of this chapter is not to determine whether there are Scriptural grounds for divorce, but to search out the Biblical attitude toward this major social problem. Would it not be wonderful if such delicate matters did not even come up? If only an answer were possible for the preacher who prayed, "Lord, just send us nice people with no problems!"

Fundamentalists hold four basic views on divorce and remarriage. First is the Jewish courtship view which says that Matthew's Gospel must be interpreted in the light of the Jewish culture of betrothal. Thus, the "fornication" of Matthew 5:31, 32 and 19:9 is premarital sex committed before the consummation of the marriage but discovered afterward or perhaps even before the marriage. Two authors who hold this interpretation are Fisher-Hunter, *The Divorce Problem*, and William Hopewell, *Marriage and Divorce*. This view essentially rules out divorce altogether.

The second view is that the word "fornication" is the generic term for immorality, which includes incest, prostitution, homosexuality, adultery, etc. Thus any type of immorality would justify divorce. Those who hold this view say Jesus is not advocating remarriage, but states it is not adultery if the wronged party insists on remarriage. This view is presented well, though briefly, by Richard DeHaan in *Marriage, Divorce, and Remarriage*. Again, it emphasizes that divorce is not encouraged, only permitted—and so is remarriage. It is the result of "hardness of heart" but, if immorality has been committed, then divorce and remarriage are not adultery. John MacArthur points out that under the Old Testament economy, an immoral mate would have been stoned to death, so Jesus gave a merciful concession to the innocent party. Under the Mosaic law the innocent one would have been free to marry anyway, being freed by the death of the guilty mate.[1]

The third view is illegal marriages to the next of kin (Lev. 18:6–18) or incestuous marriage. Divorce would then be legitimate and a permissible exception to the lifetime commitment. This view has been recently advocated by J. Carl Laney's book, *The Divorce Myth.* P. W. K. Lowther Clark and F. F. Bruce also published books supportive of this position. Other authors give variations of it, such as marriage to non-Christians or marriages of Jewish Christians to Gentile Christians.

The fourth view is that immorality on the part of either mate dissolves the marriage bond. Those who hold this view interpret "fornication" interchangeably with "adultery." This view bases its very permissive concept of remarriage on the logic that Matthew 19:9 and 5:32 should be interpreted from Deuteronomy 24:1–4 and that remarriage should not be considered as adultery at all. John Murray, professor of systematic theology at Westminster Theological Seminary, states:

> The divorce permitted or tolerated under the Mosaic economy had the effect of dissolving the marriage bond. This Mosaic permission regarding divorce is referred to in the context of this passage [Matt. 19:9] as well as in Matt. 5:31 and in the parallel passage in Mark 10:2–12 . . . the putting away sanctioned by our Lord was intended to have the same effect in the matter of dissolving the marriage tie.[2]

Guy Duty in his book, *Divorce and Remarriage,* also promotes this interpretation. Dr. Ryrie comments on this view with this criticism, "In reality this is a misuse of the passage."[3]

Whichever view the fundamentalist takes, it does not solve the issue of how to face this social problem. The real solution is not tougher divorce standards but stricter marriage standards! If as much care and thought went into the decision of marriage as most people use in purchasing a house or car, many divorces would never materialize.

One thing is certain: God hates divorce (Mal. 2:14–16)! He established marriage and the home (Gen. 2:23, 24). Jesus stated, ". . . What therefore God hath joined together, let not man put asunder" (Matt. 19:6). Not just society in general, but the church, yea, fundamental churches should set the Scriptural standard in teaching the permanency and sacredness of marriage.

The apostle Paul gave the most comprehensive instructions on divorce and remarriage in 1 Corinthians 7. In verses 8 and 9 he instructed Christian unmarrieds. Instruction for Christian husbands and wives is given in verses 10 and 11 where no divorce or remarriage to another is permitted. Then in verses 12–16 he wrote to "the rest," those couples where one mate is a believer and the other is not. Permission to break up the relationship is given. Legal action to force the continuation of the marriage is not taught: "But if the unbelieving depart, let him depart. A brother or sister is not under bondage in such cases: but God hath called us to peace" (v. 15). Whether or not Paul was allowing for remarriage is not clear from this passage; he may have had separation or divorce in mind. If remarriage is read into this, there are limitations such as 7:39, which states that remarriage is allowed only when the mate is deceased.

However, 7:27 seems to allow for remarriage without condemnation, though Dr. Ryrie holds that verse 27 only refers to a "single person (most likely an engaged couple)."[4] This interpretation does not really explain the perfect tense however.

How should fundamentalists face this growing problem? First, marriage must be presented as a *lifetime covenant*. No one should be married who does not believe this truth.

Second, marriage is a sacred covenant with God. While the state gives a license, it is to God and His laws that all must give account. Pastors should not remarry divorced people whose mates are still living no matter how "innocent" they may be for the testimony's sake. Let the civil magistrate perform the ceremony since the state took the responsibility to dissolve the marriage.

Third, the church should receive into membership those whose lives have been scarred through sin. This one sin should not be elevated above other sins. Divorced people are not to be rejected and neglected by Bible teaching churches. The very fact that deacons were to be the husbands of one wife gives evidence that there were men in the congregation who did not qualify for this high office because they were remarried. So divorced and remarried people were accepted in the New Testament church membership.

Fourth, the church should become involved in analyzing a person's past marital problems only when he is considering Christian service, such as the office of pastor or deacon. The Scriptures are clear that pastors and deacons should not be divorced and remarried (1 Tim. 3:2, 12). Most churches also hold that pastors' and deacons' wives should not be divorced and remarried (1 Tim. 3:11). If a local church passes judgment on past marital difficulties for reasons other than the consideration of choosing deacons or pastors, they do so on grounds other than direct Scriptural teaching.

Fifth, the care of divorced family members is a needed and specialized ministry. The heartache and loneliness which comes from rejection are depressing indeed. Prayer, counsel and encouragement are essential to help divorced mates and their children through this time of confusion and battered emotions. Children are often faced with painful decisions in which they must choose one parent over the other. *Divorce and the Children* by Vigeveno and Claire ought to be read by everyone who is considering divorce as the solution to a bad marriage. It is an eye-opener! A study of children from divorced families *after ten years* showed that 37 percent were still "consciously and intensely unhappy with their life in the post-divorce family."[5]

The financial burden devastates the normal family's resources. One attorney stated, "No one can afford a divorce except the very rich or the very poor."

Sixth, if a believer's marriage is broken by divorce or a divorced believer desires remarriage, the church of which he is a member must decide what to do. Usually the believer is removed from church office because of the *testimony* involved. Again, it is wise to recognize that each believer has soul liberty and may arrive at his own conviction from the study of the Word; "Let every man be fully persuaded in his own mind" (Rom. 14:5). Since sincere and reputable Bible scholars hold different views, the church should not impose one interpretation upon the believer. Only when scandal or rebellion is present does the church as a body need to act (1 Cor.

5:1–5, 11). The situation is best dealt with through pastoral counseling, compassion and prayer.

Fundamentalists must lift up the Biblical standard that marriage is sacred, ordained by God. To violate His precepts brings temporary sorrow with eternal consequences. With an estimated one million couples living together out of wedlock, Biblical standards need to be preached! With 38 percent of first marriages ending in divorce, a voice of warning needs to be sounded.[6]

Marriage and sexuality are God-designed and God-blessed (Heb. 13:4). Fundamentalists need to have happy and fulfilling homes themselves as a testimony to the unsaved community and to young Christians. Pastors' and deacons' homes should be examples (1 Tim. 3:1–12). *Reconciliation* should be taught instead of *remarriage!* Understanding and compassionate help needs to be available to those who have problems. Many people suffer in silence, even Christians. Tensions from financial disagreements and sexual maladjustments can be relieved by godly counseling. Seminars conducted by professionally trained Christian leaders can give preventative and positive instruction. (Some churches have special classes or groups designed for divorced people. Frankly, that is highly questionable as it often separates and spotlights those who need fellowship with families, not with others who are hurting.) Forgiveness should be an experience as well as a doctrine! Grace is sufficient for the wounded and lonely. God does not forsake His own.

Notes:

1. John MacArthur, Jr., *Jesus' Teaching on Divorce* (Panorama City, CA: Word of Grace Communications, 1983), p. 57.

2. John Murray, *Divorce* (Philadelphia: Presbyterian and Reformed, 1961), pp. 41, 42.

3. Charles C. Ryrie, "Biblical Teaching on Divorce and Remarriage," *Grace Theological Journal* (Fall 1982), 180.

4. Ibid., 181.

5. Lloyd Billingsley, "Bad News about the Effects of Divorce," *Christianity Today* (November 12, 1982), 84.

6. Alice Fryling, "So Many Divorces," *Eternity* (October 1980), 83.

14

Drugs:
The Insanity
of Society

The American way of life has become drug centered. A study of eighty-six households in California revealed a total of 2,539 varieties of medication with an average of 30 per household. Only one in five were prescription drugs; the others were purchased over the counter. There are drugs for just about any ailment or affliction. Twenty percent of all drugs prescribed by physicians are tranquilizers or sedatives.

Add to the pill-popping habits the use of alcohol, which is a form of escapism from reality. No wonder the youth of the nation are drug addicts. Eighty percent of our teenagers are drinking; 60 percent of the children have tried hard liquor by seventh grade, and 50 percent have tried marijuana; 25 percent of all fourth graders feel pressured by their friends to try drugs and alcohol.[1]

Add to these appalling statistics the fact that tons of poisonous narcotics are inhaled by tobacco addicts. This is done in spite of the overwhelming evidence that tobacco is a major cause of lung cancer and heart disease. Tobacco causes an estimated 300,000 premature deaths each year, one million extra cases of chronic bronchitis and emphysema, one million extra cases of peptic ulcers, and 300,000 extra coronary attacks. The cost to taxpayers is $5 billion in health care costs and about $12 billion in lost productivity and wages each year. Yet *52 million* Americans continue to smoke, polluting their bodies and polluting the air that others must breathe![2]

Another form of drug use is the taking of anabolic steroids

by athletes. The scandal in the Olympics and other sports activities causes many Americans to wonder about the sanity of the nation's prize youth. Knowing it is illegal, yet justifying its use, makes it not only a medical problem but a moral one. Kindred to this is the drug abuse among professional athletes. In 1983 forty-three players in the National Football League were treated for drug and alcohol abuse, with many more said to be dependent upon drugs, especially cocaine.[3]

The illegal drug business in this country is estimated at $79 billion! Cocaine has become a $25 billion industry and is expected to double in the next few years.[4] Every day 5,000 new users sniff a line of coke. The tie-in with organized crime makes the drug business a major social cancer. Author and correspondent Armand De Borchgrave states that it can definitely be proven that communist Fidel Castro of Cuba is financing the cocaine trade from South America to the United States. The planes which smuggle it in return with illegal guns for communist guerrillas to use in Central America.[5]

But the really frightening factor of the drug culture is not the cost to people, nor the contribution to crime, nor the broken lives and families, but it is the *religious* element. Drug users are really practicing *religion*, but it is the religion of the flesh and opens the door to satanic power. In Galatians 5:20 one of the "works of the flesh" is witchcraft. This word in the original is *pharmakeia* which means enchantment or sorcery with drugs. Revelation 9:21 describes the drug culture in the future Tribulation period and connects it with murder, immorality and thefts. (See also Revelation 18:23; 21:8; 22:15.)

Thus "trips" and mind-bending experiences are really religious experiences. God is rejected and spiritual values are repudiated. The flesh is exploited, and man's mind is set free from restraint and from revelation (the Scriptures). Galatians 5:19-21 lists the works of the flesh (of which sorcery or witchcraft is one) and says those who continue practicing these works "shall not inherit the kingdom of God." Here is the real tragedy of the drug culture: It keeps people from salvation and out of Heaven.

One of Satan's lies is that marijuana is not a serious or dangerous drug. Twenty million Americans have tried it. Ninety percent of those who attend rock festivals experiment with it. Forty-five to 70 percent of our college youth and 32 percent of our high school youth experiment with marijuana. It comes from the resin of the hemp plant call "hashish." The lowest grade of marijuana is called "bhang" and comes from the dried leaves and shoots of the uncultivated plant. It is mostly rolled into cigarettes called "reefers" or "joints." The users of this drug are motivated by curiosity, rebellion, nonconformity to authority or pressure from friends.

How dangerous is it to smoke marijuana? In July 1978 at the International Symposium on Marijuana in Reims, France, fifty researchers from fourteen countries presented new studies on how this drug injured the reproduction organs, lungs, cellular metabolism and brains of its users. In 1979 the National Institute on Drug Abuse revealed more evidence of marijuana's damage to the reproductive system. Another conference three months later at a New York medical school warned of these dangers also. Dr. Neil Solomon warns that it is most injurious to adolescent girls, affecting particularly their childbearing ability.[6]

When marijuana is smoked, the principle mind-altering cannabinoid (delta 9-THC) is stored far deep in the fatty tissues of the human brain, testes and ovaries. Effects of chronic use are evident in memory loss, lower sexual activity, even impotency and infertility. Dr. Gabriel Nahar of Columbia College of Physicians and Surgeons warns, "Today's pot smoker may not only be damaging his own mind and body, but may be playing genetic roulette and casting a shadow across children and grandchildren yet unborn."[7]

Another danger of marijuana is addiction, which often causes the user to become a thief, prostitute or pusher to keep the habit going. Furthermore, it is a channel for harder drugs. Most hard drug users started with marijuana. Also, drug use and suicide are closely linked.[8]

Hard drugs include opium, made from the poppy, with its derivatives, morphine, codeine and heroin. "Speed" is another name for benzedrine, dexedrine and the more powerful methedrine; these are "uppers." "Downers" are barbituates which depress the central nervous system. Cocaine is a stimulant and comes from the leaves of the coca tree. Another drug is LSD (lysergic acid diethylamide), a popular hallucinatory drug. Other hard drugs include peyote, mescaline and psilocybin (derived from certain mushrooms).

Fundamentalists deplore the moral and spiritual decline of America. Certainly the drug culture—both legal and illegal—is a major cause of this decline. Fundamentalists stand for these issues:

1. Stronger laws are needed to prosecute criminals who produce, distribute and use illegal drugs. These wicked criminals are not fit to live!

2. Greater efforts must be made to educate Americans concerning the dangers of drug use.

3. Christians must work as individuals to warn of and expose the spiritual and eternal consequences of drug worship.

4. It requires compassion, patience and training to reach addicts with the transforming power of Christ (Rom. 12:2). Boredom or stress may be the cause of their addiction; thus the message of the gospel may be well received.

5. Warnings and instruction need to be shared with members of fundamental churches regarding the dangers of working with people who may be addicts. Their productivity is low, and their potential for productivity is jeopardized.[9] An example of this is the aircraft crash aboard the carrier *Nimitz* in 1981. Six of the fourteen men who were killed had marijuana in their systems.[10] Other major drug users are nurses[11] and politicians and their workers.[12]

6. Christians must be careful not to become dependent on over-the-counter drugs for family use. God often uses sickness for spiritual reasons. We need to be long on prayer and self-examination and not so reliant on pills.

7. Parents of teenage drug users need prayer and support, not criticism (Gal. 6:1, 2).

8. Worldly music (including "gospel rock") should be exposed for its contribution to breaking down restraint and discipline and fostering drug use.

9. Christian schools are becoming more and more necessary in order to protect youth from the drug culture.

Education about the improper use of dangerous drugs is of vital importance to the future of our nation. Parents, teachers, youth workers, and religious leaders should all be aware of all aspects of this problem. We need to educate ourselves and then in turn better educate our children by helping them to equip themselves for the responsibility the atom and space age hold for them. It is our job, yours and mine, to help give them the fortitude, the vision, the courage and the spiritual attainment to enable them to accept and meet the challenge . . .—and it can't be done in a dream world under the effects of drugs. It will take young people with clear heads and clear consciences to carry this nation through the next decade.[13]

Notes:

1. Ann Landers, "Drugs," Houston Chronicle (September 7, 1983).

2. "Smoking" (Harrisburg, PA: Capital Blue Cross, Pennsylvania Blue Shield), p. 2.

3. Alvin P. Sanoff, "How Drugs Threaten to Ruin Pro Sports," U.S. News & World Report (September 12, 1983), 64.

4. Kurt Andersen, "Crashing on Cocaine," Time (April 11, 1983), 23.

5. Armand De Borchgrave, "The Cuban Connection," Crossfire TV (March 23, 1984).

6. Neil Solomon, "Why Is Medical Marijuana Harmful?" Houston Post (March 27, 1984).

7. Peggy Mann, "Marijuana Alert—Brain and Sex Damage," Reader's Digest (December 1979), 5.

8. Francene Klagsburn, Too Young to Die (New York: Pocket Books, 1981), p. 65.

9. John Brecher, et al., "Taking Drugs on the Job," Newsweek (August 22, 1983), 57.

10. Ibid.

11. Marcia Dunn, "Programs Set up to Help Nurses Fight Addiction," Houston Chronicle (February 19, 1984).

12. Sally Squires, "Cocaine Use Is a Fact of Life on Capitol Hill," Houston Chronicle (January 29, 1984).

13. Fred G. Clark and Richard S. Rimanoczy, The Christian School Tackles the Root of Drug Abuse (Buena Park, CA: California Free Enterprise Association).

15

Euthanasia:
The Rejected
of Society

The humanist view of a living creature, in particular a human being, contradicts the Judeo-Christian ethic. No life should be terminated on social or medical grounds unless that person has taken the life of another (Gen. 9:6). Euthanasia, which means "good death" is the justification for terminating the life of the elderly or the hopelessly diseased or deformed. Dr. C. Everett Koop, Surgeon General of the United States, comments that these humanistic reasons have very little to do with medical limitations but have to do with staff decisions based upon the social problems of the patient in question, such as visitation by the family, the number of nursing hours required per week, etc.[1]

Mercy killing, its advocates claim, is a blessing to the oppressed, not homicide. The problem is *when* does a person need such "mercy" and *who* should play God and make such a decision?

Two types of euthanasia are voluntary and involuntary. The former leaves the ultimate decision to the patient; e.g., the physician leaves the pill bottle near for an overdose. The involuntary decision is made by the physician or family members without the consent of the patient.[2] Such patients include deformed fetuses and the terminally ill.

This active euthanasia should be considered homicide.[3] It completely rejects the possibility that the Lord could and sometimes does raise up hopelessly ill people. Furthermore, it does not consider that God may have a purpose for suffering and illness. It forces all decisions into the pigeon-holed mentality of modern science and its humanistic assumptions. About four out of five people now die in a hospital or nursing home; family responsibility is shifting to professionals.[4]

Euthanasia is not the same as the prayerful and thoughtful planning for death which prohibits extraordinary lifesaving devices. A wise and popular document is the "Living Will" which a person files with his or her physician and family. This authorizes the physician not to prolong life by costly mechanical means. To prolong comatose patients' lives indefinitely on life-support systems does not please God or man. The Karen Quinlan case is an example where all vital signs were gone, yet doctors were legally bound to continue life-support systems until complicated legal questions were settled by the courts. Because these machines can prolong visible signs of life even after the brain has ceased to function, thirty-one states now use brain wave tests to determine death.

But situations of mechanically prolonged lives are not really the issue. The issue is, Should society do away with unwanted people? Should medical help be withheld from the deformed and the aged? The same mentality that has created the abortion scandal promotes euthanasia. William Price of Bible Fellowship Inc. observes the following national trend:

INFANTICIDE AND EUTHANASIA are now being practiced at ever increasing rates. The newborn infant who was born less than perfect and the elderly infirm have become the next targets for death selection.

The John Hopkins Medical Center enthusiastically endorsed and has promoted the practice of infanticide. Professors Raymond Duff and A.G.M. Campbell from the Yale University School of Medicine announced in a recent New England Journal of Medicine article that over a two year period 14% of the deaths in the Newborn Intensive Care Nursery were deaths that they *permitted to happen* because it was their considered judgment after much discussion with the family that these children had "lives not worth living."

Perhaps you heard of the recent case in Indiana where a baby born with Down's Syndrome and a malformed esophagus died of starvation. This death did not occur in some under developed Third World country. It occurred in

Indiana. His parents decided to let him die rather than authorize a corrective operation or even permit intravenous feeding because he had Down's Syndrome.

Dr. C. Everett Koop, the Surgeon General of the United States, reports that 80% of a group of pediatric surgeons when asked, "Do you believe that the life of every newborn infant should be saved if it is within our ability to do so" answered *no*. That same study found that 76% would acquiesce in a parental refusal to allow low-risk yet life-saving surgery for a mentally retarded infant.

The November 1979 issue of Readers' Digest reported on the growing non-treatment of fever in extended-care facilities for the elderly. In England the cut-off age for receiving government funding for dialysis treatment is 52 years of age. This trend is spreading.

For the first time since Nazi Germany we are witnessing a regression to death technology and to state sanctioned, credentialed, exterminative medicine. History documents that legalized abortion and euthanasia preceded the Holocaust.[5]

The nation was shocked when the governor of Colorado, Richard Lamm, stated that the elderly who are terminally ill have a "duty to die." This is a humanistic attitude, and it sounds like Nazi Germany.[6]

The question of whether an individual can refuse medical treatment is still unsettled. Often institutions fear malpractice suits, so treatment is forced on patients. More complicated is the issue of denying food to dying patients or to seriously ill infants (362,000 are born each year). The costs of prolonging life in the seriously ill are astronomical, but withholding food is different. Dr. Koop states that "withholding fluids or nourishment at any time is an immoral act."[7]

One reason to prolong life is to provide organs for transplants. This can be helpful when the patient is an accident victim. Also a pregnant woman can be allowed to bring an unborn infant to maturity.[8] The issue can be summarized as making the distinction between prolonging the act of dying and protecting the act of living. Society must put a high value on life.

Fundamentalists repudiate the humanistic philosophy that man is only an animal and should be treated with a barnyard mentality. Sociobiology, the new science which is growing in influence in the medical world, promotes abortion, euthanasia and the killing of malformed infant children.[9] The definition of sociobiology is the systematic study of biology as the basic force of all social behavior. This has developed from the assumed theory of evolution. Its most noted publicist is Edward O. Wilson of Harvard. Commenting on Wilson's views, Ray Bohlin states, "To sociobiology, perhaps Hitler's ideas were only forty years ahead of their time, although some of his methods may seem a bit crude."[10]

Wilson blatantly judges all men to be purely materialistic. He states, "If human kind evolved by Darwinian natural selection, genetic change and environmental necessity, not God, made the species."[11] When there is no God, there is no morality, no ethics and no eternity. Bohlin well exhorts Bible-believers:

> . . . We also have a responsibility to tear down strongholds raised against the knowledge of God. Surely the naturalistic philosophy of secular sociobiology is such a stronghold, so we must take strong exception to it.[12]

Fundamentalists repudiate euthanasia as anti-Biblical and humanistic.

Notes:

1. Koop, "Abortion and the Future," p. 11.
2. W. Merwin Forbes, "Euthanasia," *Spire* (Summer 1981), 8.
3. Ibid.
4. Susan Tifft, "Debate on the Boundary of Life," *Time* (April 11, 1983), 68.
5. William Price, *Abortion: It's Killing America* (Dallas: Bible Fellowship), pp. 2, 3.
6. Tifft, p. 68.
7. Ibid., p. 70.
8. Ray Bohlin, "Sociobiology: Cloned from the Gene Cult," *Christianity Today* (January 23, 1981), 16.
9. Ibid., p. 18.
10. Ibid.
11. Ibid., p. 19.
12. Ibid.

16

Femininity vs. Feminism: The Struggle in Society

Is there a difference between femininity and feminism? Yes! The former is God's plan in operation, while the latter is the world's. The first is freedom and contentment, and the second is rebellion and slavery.

It is true that many cultures, past and present, have taken advantage of women. It is Christianity which has freed women from oppression and prejudice. The Bible teaches women are *equal* with men in the salvation experience (Gal. 3:28), in spirituality (Eph. 2:18) and in sexual activity and authority (1 Cor. 7:3, 4).

But the Bible also teaches she is the weaker vessel (1 Pet. 3:7), second in order of position (1 Cor. 11:3; 1 Tim. 2:13), not in authority over the husband (Col. 3:18), not in authority over men in the local church (1 Tim. 2:12), and should be dedicated to homemaking and caring for children (1 Tim. 2:15; Titus 2:4, 5).

The differences in the emotional and physical makeups of women and men does not mean inferiority. John Leo in *Time* reviews the book, *Femininity*, by famed feminist Susan Brownmiller with this notation:

> The book points out that physiology can sometimes influence function: small, light bones and agile fingers give women a greater aptitude for such traditional work as weaving, sewing, knitting, making pottery, sowing, planting and

121

weeding, she writes. Men's bodies are more fit for "clearing the land and breaking the soil." A woman's hand makes a poor fighting fist, she writes, but is good for the assembly of small parts, exacting kitchen chores, film editing, secretarial work and neurosurgery.[1]

The basis of feminism seeks equality even when there is none. Some even believe that taking the husband's name in marriage "submerges their identities in those of their husbands" (*A Feminist Manifesto*). So the use of Ms. had become popular. It is true that women have been taken advantage of in areas such as wages. In 1982 the average for women's wages was 63 cents for each dollar men were paid.[2] And women are often brutalized sexually, both legally and illegally, which is deplorable!

But the most grievous idea that the feminist movement has promoted is that being a wife and mother is inferior. It is the highest, noblest and most satisfying career! And it is God's design and order. That does not mean that He does not lead certain women into careers of engineering, education, medicine, politics, law, etc., but homemaking is a blessed and satisfying lifetime work.

In conjunction with the rise of feminism, the Biblical writings of the apostle Paul have been questioned and even attacked. Paul Jewett of Fuller Seminary (*Man as Male and Female*) and Virginia Mollenkott, professor of English at William Peterson College (*Women, Men, and the Bible*) are two of the most notable critics. Their basis for rejecting the apostle's teaching on women and submission is that Paul was warped by his rabbinical heritage. H. Wayne House in his analysis of this criticism of Paul states, "According to Mollenkott this contradiction in the apostle is because of his rabbinical training. . . . Also Jewett accepts this rabbinic spell on Paul."[3]

Obviously such viewpoints conflict with the orthodox position on the verbal inspiration of the Scriptures. House comments, "Scripture is presented by many evangelical feminists as having erroneous teaching on the role of women."[4] Such challenges to the authority of the Bible must be dismissed by fundamentalists as heretical.

The fact that the apostle Paul gave instructions about the cultural idiosyncrasies in the ancient city of Corinth shows that women did speak and pray in the public worship service (1 Cor. 11:5). First

Corinthians 14:34 is not to be interpreted that women were never to speak in the service. Kenneth Gangel thinks this "silence" means open discussion or dialogue in the public service was prohibited; the women were to wait until they were home with their husbands.[5] This seems to be a reasonable explanation since the apostolic churches segregated the sexes after the pattern of the synagogue.

Key women were acknowledged as leaders by the apostle Paul; e.g., Phebe (Rom. 16:1), Euodias and Syntyche (Phil. 4:2) and Priscilla (Acts 18:26). These faithful women were appreciated and used in the gospel ministry. The history of the church would be scarred and left with wide gaps without the countless number of godly women such as Lydia (Acts 16:14), who opened her home and heart to the cause of evangelism and missions, and the sacrificing Dorcas, who was full of good works (Acts 9:36).

While there are limitations in Christian service for women, there are also great opportunities. Missions, teaching, music and administration in Christian schools are but a few of these.

Praise God for godly women, both those who serve in specialized vocations and those who support their husbands in his calling. Fundamentalists do not consider these treasured women as inferior!

Fundamentalists recognize the God-designed differences between men and women. They accept *God's order*, not only in creation, but in the home and in the local church as binding and needful. The modern feminist movement is anti-Biblical and illogical. It should be rejected and exposed for its humanistic philosophy as evidenced in the Equal Rights Amendment. Tim LaHaye raises some serious questions about the ERA. He states:

> The Equal Rights Amendment is a good illustration of the movement itself. Ratified quickly by the Senate and House of Representatives, in 1972, it was railroaded through thirty-four states before serious questions surfaced. Would the Equal Rights Amendment legalize homosexuality, making it possible for homosexual school-teachers to flaunt their position as an optional life-style, in our public schools? Would it make it impossible to refuse to hire a known homosexual or force employers, through affirmative action and job quotas, to fire heterosexuals and hire homosexuals? Would landlords have to rent to known

homosexuals? Would the courts have to record homosexual marriages and give known homosexuals child custody? Would girls be eligible for the draft against their will, and would women be forced into combat? Many lawyers responded with a resounding yes! including former senator Sam Ervin (Democrat from North Carolina), known and respected on both sides of the aisle as a constitutional authority. Concurring statements appeared in the prestigious *Yale Law Journal* and *Harvard Law Journal.*[6]

Fundamentalists defend the traditional family as Biblical and moral. God in His wisdom has established order in His creation, and fundamentalists teach it and practice it because it is right. An excellent book for further study on this subject is *Women and the Word of God—A Response to Biblical Feminism* by Susan T. Foh (Presbyterian and Reformed Publishing Co.).

Notes:

1. John Leo, "The Comeback of Womanly Wiles," *Time* (January 30, 1984), 32.
2. Ted Gest, "Battle of the Sexes over Comparable Worth," *U. S. News & World Report* (February 20, 1984), 73.
3. H. Wayne House, "Paul, Women, and Contemporary Evangelical Feminism, *Bibliotheca Sacra* (January—March, 1979), 43.
4. Ibid., p. 45.
5. Kenneth O. Gangel, "Biblical Feminism and Church Leadership," *Bibliotheca Sacra* (January—March 1983), 58.
6. Tim LaHaye, *The Battle for the Family* (Old Tappan, NJ: Fleming H. Revell, 1982), p. 137.

17

Gambling:
the Weakness
in Society

The problem of gambling exceeds the most exasperating limits. More than 60 percent of all American adults engage in some kind of gambling. The amount spent is $4,500 annually for every man, woman and child. Most of the $32 billion a year wagered with professional bet takers and numbers racketeers is illegal.[1]

What these amazing statistics reveal is that the corruption of this society is far more extensive than we realize. And it is increasing! The increase in televised athletic events is pushing sports betting (estimated at $60-75 billion annually) to even greater highs, exceeded only by the traffic in illegal drugs (estimated at $79 billion a year).

The crime rate is affected by gambling due to bribes to police and politicians. Government intrusion into the gambling world with state-run lotteries and racing softens the public's sensitivity toward this menace. In addition, some church organizations, especially the Roman Catholic church, sponsor gambling events. These further contribute to the breakdown of public morality.

But the greatest tragedy is the addiction of so many citizens: 12 million compulsive gamblers! Like alcoholic addiction, only when these sick and sin-dominated addicts reach the "desperation state" can they change and be helped through counseling. The real answer, of course, is the grace and power of Jesus Christ to change the sinner (2 Cor. 5:17).

Gambling is the game of chance. Not skill nor training and usually not even experience determine the outcome of the game. Gambling is a form of covetousness, which the Bible calls idolatry (Col. 3:5). It is born from greed and a get-rich-fast mentality.

What attitude should the fundamentalist have toward gambling? While no direct Scriptural prohibition is found, the Bible is clear that chance, greed and covetousness are sinful.

> Perverse disputings of men of corrupt minds, and destitute of the truth, supposing that gain is godliness: from such withdraw thyself.
> But godliness with contentment is great gain.
> For we brought nothing into this world, and it is certain we can carry nothing out.
> And having food and raiment let us be therewith content.
> But they that will be rich fall into temptation and a snare, and into many foolish and hurtful lusts, which drown men in destruction and perdition.
> For the love of money is the root of all evil: which while some coveted after, they have erred from the faith, and pierced themselves through with many sorrows (1 Tim. 6:5-10).

> A faithful man shall abound with blessings: but he that maketh haste to be rich shall not be innocent (Prov. 28:20).

> Labour not to be rich: cease from thine own wisdom.
> Wilt thou set thine eyes upon that which is not? for riches certainly make themselves wings; they fly away as an eagle toward heaven (Prov. 23:4, 5).

> Jesus said unto him, It is written again, Thou shalt not tempt the Lord thy God (Matt. 4:7).

The spirit of gambling is contrary to trusting the sovereign Lord of the universe, Who controls all things but does not cause all things (Rom. 8:28-31). Gambling is an offense to Him Who gives us every good gift, even salvation and eternal life in Heaven.

Notes:

1. James Mann, "Gambling Rage—Out of Control?" *U. S. News & World Report* (May 30, 1983), 27.

2. Ibid., p. 29.

18

Genetic Engineering: The Fear of Society

Within the scientific world, genetic engineering has sparked more controversy than anything since nuclear experiments began in 1940. Significant advances in this area were made in 1973 with the discovery of ways to chop up genetic material and put it back together. This made it possible to splice together material from different species, forming a new set of genes with unique hereditary traits.[1]

Some major benefits have resulted from this research. One is the brain hormone, somatostatin, which is valuable for medical science. This research has also made possible the revolutionary development of artificial insemination, sperm banks, in vitro fertilization (test tube babies), embryonic sex changes, surrogate mothers, amniocentesis, recombinant DNA and cloning research.

One of the basic physical dangers which the scientific community must face is that artificial, genetic species may upset the balance of nature.[2] Another danger which may be far greater is the spiritual aspect; that is, the disregard for traditional family moral values and the sanctity of life.

How critical is this new genetic engineering to society? Here are some recent newspaper headlines: "Putting Value on Human Life Worries Some"; "No Clear Fraud Evidence Found in Clone Research"; "Religionists vs. Scientists—Views on Ethics of Human Genetic Engineering Differ"; "Congressional Guru of Genetic Engineering Tomorrow, and How Today's Congress Should Deal with It"; "Facing the Issues—Genetic Engineering"; "Playing God? Gene splicing stirs debate that may change science, humanity"; "Genetic technique would let parents choose child's sex"; "Choosing the sex of children may become possible"; "High-Tech Babies"; "Will gene splicing be worth the risks?"; "Religious leaders ask federal ban on gene engineering"; "Test tube fertilization might be more effective than nature, doctors say"; "Test-tube fertilization criticized by Vatican as immoral practice"; "Are human beings more than the chemicals they are made of?"

When genetic engineering aids medical science to cure genetic disease and to give hope for those with infertility problems, its results are indeed worthy. But the potential for abuse is frightening. "Gene splicing" to improve looks or brains, called "germline intervention" (when genes are inserted into the sperm of men or the eggs of women whose cells fuse at fertilization), ceases to be medical and becomes philosophical. It is playing God! A congressional investigation and a presidential commission have studied this subject to determine guidelines.

And there is no easy solution. Over 2,000 diseases are related to inherited genetic defects. The enormity of the challenge can be seen as scientists chart the genes and their functions and study DNA units that govern the development of the body organs and tissues. It is thought that the human body may have as many as 100,000 genes and only about 500 genes have been identified in their repositories, the chromosomes. By the end of this century all of them should be identified.[3]

The presidential commission has attempted to put these conflicts into perspective. It stated:

> Stopping any enterprise out of fear of potential evil not only deprives humanity of the fruits of new findings but also stifles strong impulses for innovation and change. Nevertheless, the technological allure of gene splicing ought not to be allowed to blind society to the need for sober judgments, publicly arrived at, about whether there are instances in which the price of going ahead with an experiment or an innovation will be higher than the price paid by stopping the work.[4]

A sobering thought is put forth by Paul Schimmel, Professor of Biochemistry and Biophysics at Massachusetts Institute of Technology: "This technology which gives scientists the ability to manipulate genes and heredity has to do with the *process of life itself*. That means it affects everyone."[5] Unfortunately, the scientific world cannot be trusted, as evidenced by the Nazis' experimentations and the communists' use of mental hospitals to squash dissenters. Man is viewed as an animal, only to be developed and manipulated. His spiritual nature and his eternal destiny are ignored or denied. Genetic engineering, if not directed or limited, could endanger the very existence of man as a free moral agent. Children would be selected like the purchase of a new car with all its options. Even now the use of surrogate mothers reminds this author of horse breeding on the farm! There is no place for God or His will. Man wants to control his own destiny. He forgets that the family is not a human convenience, but is of divine origin.

Perhaps the most eery of the engineering methods is cloning. Cloning is production of exact replicas of certain people. This, of course, violates the basic truth that "children are an heritage of the LORD" (Ps. 127:3). Fundamentalists ought to protest this wicked, humanistic device, even though it is very unlikely humans can ever be cloned.

Likewise, the process of amniocentesis can be dangerous when embryonic diseases are detected, not just for correction, but to promote abortion. The procedure should not be abused.

Research into recombinant DNA (deoxyribonucleic acid, in which the chemistry of heredity is spelled out) can be valuable in treating certain maladies. Interferon research is one possible breakthrough in the cancer battle. While the process is time-consuming, it is promising.[6] The production of insulin is another example of medical assistance. The increase in plant production through nitrogen fixation could help relieve the world's hunger problems. But fundamentalists should warn against any restructuring of humans, for God made man in *His* image (Gen. 1:27).

Michael Hamilton comments on the ethical tensions which arise over these experiments with this insight:

> Faced with the obvious dangers of this scientific course, some have demanded a halt to further technological and

research developments until the effect of present programs can be more fully assessed. . . . However our society has decided to risk both the known and the unknown dangers of abortion and artificial insemination because of the known advantages. I expect that our society will not object in principle to *in vitro* fertilization, cloning, and the transfer of pregnancies from one womb to another or from an *in vitro* state to a womb. But the experiments necessary to perfect such techniques may well entail ethical risks that are unacceptable to us. . . . However, abuses will inevitably occur.[7]

Christians sometimes react negatively to innovations without cause. After all telephones, vaccines and microfilms are blessings to humanity. Carl Henry (reporting on a Conference on Human Engineering) advocated that "the Christian Church should oppose research only when it infringes upon biblical principles or is unworthy."[8] Charles Smith, Professor of Theology at Grace Theological Seminary, lists several wise and godly considerations which help Christians have the proper attitude toward this issue.

First, the Bible teaches that God has given man dominion over physical creation (Gen. 1:28). It is fitting and proper for man to attempt to correct physical and genetic defects— whether by surgery or other means which are consistent with the dignity and sanctity of human life (Gen. 9:6; Jas. 3:9).

Second, human life begins at conception, or at least at the first cell divisions (the beginning of replication), and is worthy of the utmost care and respect during all the stages of human development and aging. In the governmental laws established for the Israelite theocracy, God even decreed the punishment of one who might accidently cause an abortion (miscarriage, Ex. 21:22, 25).

Third, it would be sinful to be unmoved and unconcerned about the defects, mutations, and diseases which plague mankind (I John 3:17). The parable of the Good Samaritan illustrates the proper attitude toward the consequences of sin.

Fourth, God has stated His desire for men and women to procreate and for the children to be raised within a loving and instructive family relationship involving marriage and commitment (Gen. 1:28, 2:24; Eph. 5:22—6:4; et al).

Fifth, adoption is a biblically approved concept. God has adopted believers as His Sons (Gal. 3:26—4:7). Jesus himself was adopted by Joseph (Lk. 3:23).[9]

Fundamentalists must not fight medical and scientific progress which does not violate basic morality and the dignity of man. But we should oppose anything which challenges the sanctity of life or destroys the family unit.

Notes:

1. Paul Schimmel, "Genetic Engineering: Blessing or Curse?" *Christianity Today* (June 2, 1978), 15.

2. Ibid., p. 16.

3. Bob Tutt, "Gene Splicing Stirs Debate That May Change Science, Humanity," *Houston Chronicle* (July 31, 1983).

4. Ibid.

5. Schimmel, p. 16.

6. John P. Abbott, "Biotechnology," *Shell News* (January 1984), 14, 15.

7. Michael P. Hamilton, *The New Genetics and the Future of Man* (Grand Rapids: Wm. B. Eerdmans, 1971), pp. 10, 11.

8. Carl F. H. Henry, "Human Engineering," *Christianity Today* (September 12, 1975), 48.

9. Charles R. Smith, "The Manipulation of Human Reproduction," *Spire* (Summer 1981), 4.

19

Homosexuality:
The Menace
to Society

While fundamentalists agree on the fact that homosexuality is sinful, opinions differ on how these unfortunate people can or should be treated as a social problem. Should homosexuals be allowed to teach in public schools or to work in factories? To what do their "rights" extend, and where do they cease? Are they citizens with voting rights? Should they have their own churches, bars and bathhouses? Is it wrong to single out homosexuality as more reprehensible than other forms of sexual misbehavior?

The Scriptures clearly teach that sexual perversion is wicked (Rom. 1:24–32; 1 Cor. 6:9, 10; 1 Tim. 1:10). But to the fundamentalist, it is not just the sexual perversion which the homosexual practices that is so abominable; it is that he or she often preys on the innocent, even youngsters. How can any right-thinking, decent-minded citizen or parent allow homosexuals to work in positions where they come in contact with young people? Even if a homosexual teacher does not attempt to seduce children, he is a bad role model. Fundamentalists must speak out against the blatant attempts of perverts to change laws and gain "rights" which endanger the moral safety of our youth.

Fundamentalists are accused of an unloving spirit and unbending attitude. But it should be pointed out that God detests homosexuality! In His instruction to Israel, the Lord said, "Do not lie with a man as one lies with a woman; that is detestable" (Lev. 18:22, NIV; the King James Version uses the word "abomination"). Fundamentalists believe that what the Lord detests, they should detest! The Hebrew word *toeva* means repulsive; it is used in Isaiah 1:13 and Ezekiel 16:50 in reference to Sodomites.

Some homosexuals even marry each other! To top this, some denominations (e.g., Presbyterians, Methodists, Episcopalians) accept and even ordain homosexuals. The National Council of Churches has postponed its decision as to whether it should accept the membership of the Metropolitan Community Church.

Several years ago I heard the Reverend Troy Perry, founder and one of the leaders of the homosexual Metropolitan Community Church, at Iowa State University (seminar on sexuality). He claimed that he was a graduate of Moody Bible Institute and had been a fundamentalist at one time. He had the audacity to claim that God had predestined that he should be homosexual. This is blasphemy! This perverted church does not point homosexuals to Christ, but comforts them and gives them a sense of acceptance.[1]

It is vital for fundamentalists to understand the importance of *acceptance* for homosexuals. This is why gay organizations are so popular with them. Somewhere in the perverted psyche of homosexuals there is the cry for acceptance. Thus, politicians and church leaders and others who give them respectability are really doing them a terrible disservice, for they are encouraging them in their quest for acceptance.

What causes this perversion? Homosexuals want to believe it is *genetics*, but there is simply no medical proof for this.[2] Most experts believe it is the lack of a balanced, normal family life in the formative years which brings fears of the opposite sex. Psychologist Clyde Narramore states: "If parents are not well adjusted, abnormal and disturbed feelings can develop in the child. . . . Children also need good models. . . . They need to be with both peers and adults who are comfortable with their own sexual identity and who can help children feel good about them too."[3]

Educators and counselors report that often homosexuals come from homes where the mothers dominate or where the fathers are hostile or detached. While this does not *cause* homosexuality in either males or females, it is often a factor.

Perverted sexuality—like all sin—is the *choice* of the sinner. Lust, intrigue and desire for the bizarre are temptations which draw wicked people to wicked actions (James 1:13–16). Since perversion comes by choice, it can be rejected by choice. First Peter 2:11 says, ". . . Abstain from fleshly lusts, which war against the soul." Paul wrote to Timothy, "Flee also youthful lusts . . ." (2 Tim. 2:22).

Complicating the homosexual life are the unique diseases which plague practicing homosexuals. The most notable is AIDS (acquired immune deficiency syndrome) which has no known cure at this time. Unfortunately this dreaded disease can be spread to the general public through contaminated blood.[4] Perhaps this awesome, fatal disease comes from God's direct judgment. At any rate, it has brought great fear and some restraint to the homosexual community.

Homosexuals want society to think they are mostly couples who live "normal lives." But the facts just do not support this. One-half of the homosexual men have affairs with hundreds of other men; 40 percent have more than 500 sex partners. Twenty-five percent of these adults have performed sexual acts with boys under sixteen years of age. Two-thirds have had venereal disease at least once. Lesbians (female homosexuals) are less promiscuous, but all have very low self-esteem and many are suicidal. Twenty percent of the homosexual men have attempted suicide.[5]

With these emotional and physical problems, why in the world are homosexuals called *gay?* These misguided misfits in society are miserable, and this drives them to the bizarre.

In their quest for acceptance, homosexuals have attempted to reinterpret the Bible. They claim the sin of Sodom was not homo-sexuality but inhospitality. They say "against nature" in Romans 1:26 does not apply to them because homosexual acts are "natural" to them. Or they say that the apostle Paul was not condemning "normal homosexuality" but rather the pagan Greek practice of pederasts and catamites. They point out that Jesus never taught against homosexuality. (He didn't have to. The Jews of His day did not even consider practicing it.) Simple, honest exegesis of the Scriptures leads to the conclusion that homosexuality is sin. Ukleja calls it "intrinsic evil."[6] Any who practice it or condone its practice offend God. The practicing homosexual cannot be considered a saved person (1 Cor. 6:9, 10).

These recent trends to give respectability to this ancient wicked-ness are regrettable and deplorable: (1) The decision of the Amer-ican Psychiatric Association to remove homosexuality from its list of mental disorders; (2) articles in national magazines such as *Woman's Day, Time, Newsweek* and religious publications which give the impression of respectability; (3) politicians who seek and accept the endorsement of homosexual organizations; (4) liberal church organizations which accept and recognize (and even ordain) homosexuals; (5) some new evangelicals (e.g., Letha Scanzoni and Virginia Mollenkott) who want to compromise on this issue and suggest tolerance and even acceptance of this sin as an "alternate life style."

Can homosexuals be reached for Christ? Of course, but with great difficulty. Bible truth cannot be sweetened or softened. The repudiation of homosexuality is clear. Fundamentalists must have compassion on these trapped souls. Their perversion does not exclude them from the gospel! Fundamentalists must not fail to see these people as a mission field. It is a difficult ministry with very low results, as I can personally report. But the gospel is the *power of God* unleashed! It must be preached to homosexuals even though churches must never allow membership to them until there is evidence of repentance and regeneration. Fundamentalists must also warn society against any intrusion of homosexuals into certain areas of the nation's professions and public life. They are a menace to society, and their sin is an abomination to God.

Notes:

1. I. M., "Metropolitan Community Church: Deception Discovered," *Christianity Today* (April 26, 1974), 13.

2. "The Homosexual in America," *Time* (January 21, 1966), 41.

3. Clyde M. Narramore, *The Psychosexual Development of Children* (Rosemead, CA: The Narramore Christian Foundation, 1984), pp. 2–5.

4. James Mann, "An AIDS Scare Hits Nation's Blood Supply," *U. S. News & World Report* (July 25, 1983), 71.

5. "A New Kinsey Report," *Time* (July 17, 1978), 53.

6. P. Michael Ukleja, "Homosexuality in the New Testament," *Bibliotheca Sacra* (October—December 1983), 353.

20

Hunger and Poverty: The Needy of Society

What causes poverty and hunger? Not one thing, but many. The eighteenth-century English economist, Thomas Malthus, concluded that the growth of the population will always tend to outgrow the food supply. Only wars and famines limit the number of poor. His solution was very naive, for he advocated the neglect of the poor and urged them to refrain from sexual activity!

Aside from particular famines caused by wars, droughts or catastrophe, no one can deny that *too many people* cause poverty and hunger. Only population control, especially in Third World countries, can give long-range relief. But the problem and the solution are hard to separate, for, "Poverty breeds babies."[1]

Some self-styled experts accuse the United States and other industrial nations as causing world hunger. They say it is our political or economic policies which directly or indirectly deny millions the opportunity to receive sufficient food.[2] One such critic is Ronald Sider, former professor at Messiah College, now with Eastern Baptist Seminary. Sider has wide influence as President of Evangelicals for Social Action, as well as through his writings, such as *Rich Christians in an Age of Hunger*. Sider lays a guilt trip on anyone who enjoys financial success and prosperity. He has developed a "doctrine of judgment and of God's call to repentance."[3]

Sider challenges churches in America on the ethics of building church buildings ($3.9 billion was spent in the 1970s) when "over 2.5 billion people have not yet heard of Jesus Christ and when one billion people were starving or malnourished."[4] Sider makes another sweeping indictment in the following statement:

> Present economic relationships in the worldwide body of Christ are unbiblical, sinful, a hindrance to evangelism, and a desecration of the body and blood of Jesus Christ. The dollar value of food North Americans throw in the garbage each year equals about one-fifth of the total income of Africa's 120 million Christians. It is a sinful abomination for a small fraction of the world's Christians living in the Northern Hemisphere to grow richer year by year while our brothers and sisters in Christ in the Third World ache and suffer for lack of minimal health care, minimal education, and, in thousands and thousands of cases, just enough food to escape starvation.[5]

What is wrong with the views of Sider and his fellow new evangelicals? First of all, it may well be that God has blessed the United States with prosperity because of His divine purpose. America's freedom to proclaim the gospel and her treatment of the Jews are two possible reasons. To blame this nation's churches for not feeding less prosperous "Christians" is preposterous. Another fallacy of Sider's view is his failure to recognize that many nations' plight and poverty are brought upon themselves due to religious and cultural practices. In India, for instance, the people will not eat their cattle; Arab countries have horrendous sanitation. Robert Frykenberg criticizes Sider for not understanding that inefficient governmental organizations are a major contributing cause of hunger. He further criticizes Sider by accusing him of failing to do the following:

> . . . to delve into Scriptural and phenomenological *causes* of hunger. He also totally ignores the power of evil and the social consequences of inhumanity and sin, especially as these are manifested in both Christian and non-Christian, rich and poor alike. Whatever remains of the original divine image in which God fashioned man, sheer human wickedness can result in deeds of inhumanity and can thwart man's best efforts to alleviate the human condition.[6]

Frykenberg continues his rejection of Sider's simplicity and theological assumptions. He states:

Thus, when Ronald Sider writes about India's starving millions and postulates the scenario of an Indian prime minister attempting nuclear blackmail of wealthy nations in order to feed the starving people of India, his perception becomes ludicrous. . . . But what is not understood is that: (1) at least 300 million other people in India have never lived so well or had it so good; . . . (2) millions are unbelievably affluent, thousands of them millionaires and powerful landlords; (3) one of the world's largest, best, and oldest standing armies and even larger numbers of peace officials; . . . (4) some hundred million of these same people are esteemed "untouchable"; and (5) hundreds (even thousands) of distinct communities (castes, etc.) are separated from each other by strict pollution rules. India is not starving; rather *one portion of the people of India* is starving while another portion lives in super abundance.[7]

It should be added to the above perceptive criticism of Sider and other new evangelicals that the inequities of India's caste system are due to wicked paganism. Rebellion against God and His revelation is the root cause. Why blame America and American Christians whose free enterprise system gives freedom to work and live and prosper?

John Witmer of Dallas Theological Seminary, in his review of radical new evangelical Tom Hanks's articles on the poor in the left-wing evangelical periodicals *Sojourners* and *The Other Side*, makes this comment:

The articles provide a good illustration of a one-sided approach to the teachings of the Bible. . . . Hanks and others who echo his point of view need to stop and think about their own situations. If God had not enabled some of His children to accumulate wealth and then to disperse it in response to God's leading, the Latin American Biblical Seminary where Hanks ministers would not exist. As a result his position is kind of like biting the hand that feeds him. The same thing is true of both *Sojourners* and *The Other Side*, since the magazines are able to continue publication only because of the gifts of Christians beyond subscriptions.[8]

The fact is American Christians do give substantially to the poor and hungry of the world through government agencies as well as contributions to private agencies. In January 1984 United States Secretary of State George Shultz testified that the United States was giving a $500 million economic package to Africa over the next five years.[9]

The United Nations, the Red Cross, CARE and scores of other organizations aid in disasters and calamities. Though these are perhaps wasteful and slow at times, some help is given. Unfortunately, many countries do not help themselves or prepare themselves for difficulties.

The question must be faced: Should fundamentalists help feed the hungry of the world? The answer from the Bible is NO. The reasons are several; note these:

1. Jesus said the poor would remain in society (Matt. 26:11; Mark 14:7; John 12:3). So, while their plight may be alleviated, it will not be erased until Jesus returns to establish His Kingdom.

2. In relation to the parable of the unjust steward in Luke 16, "No word is found here concerning the believer's responsibility outside the circle of disciples. The elimination of poverty or the equalizing of wealth was not Jesus' goal."[10]

3. The greatest gift which can be given to the poor is the gospel (Ps. 112:9; 2 Cor. 9:9).

4. Giving to the poor is commendable, but it is not a substitute for the gospel (Matt. 19:21; Luke 14:13; Gal. 2:10).

5. Individual poverty is not necessarily an indication of failure or God's displeasure (Luke 6:20).

6. God will never let His saints suffer unless His purpose has eternal reasons (Ps. 37:25; Rom. 8:28).

Fundamentalists do need to be aware of the terrible physical suffering in the world. Fifty percent of the world's people go to bed hungry and 10,000 die each day of starvation. But even greater is the *spiritual* deprivation; over 50 percent of the world's population have never heard of the Bread of Life.

Fundamentalists believe that the suffering of the poor does not constitute a call to action to rid the world of that situation. But individuals should assist wherever possible as compassionate citizens. And certainly fundamental churches must not neglect the needy in their own midst (James 2:14–16).

Notes:

1. Bee-lan Wang, "World Hunger: Starve It or Feed It?" *Christianity Today* (September 5, 1980), 20.

2. David Olson, "Christians in a Hungry World," *Christianity Today* (March 10, 1978), 17.

3. Ibid.

4. Ronald J. Sider, "Cautions against Ecclesiastical Elegance," *Christianity Today* (August 17, 1979), 15.

5. Ibid., p. 16.

6. Robert E. Frykenberg, "World Hunger: Food Is Not the Answer," *Christianity Today* (December 11, 1981), 36.

7. Ibid., p. 37.

8. John A. Witmer, "Periodical Reviews," *Bibliotheca Sacra* (July—September 1981), 267.

9. S. M. Khalid, " 'America Responds' to Hungry, Dying," *U.S.A. Today* (January 31, 1984).

10. Charles C. Ryrie, "Perspectives on Social Issues, Part III," *Bibliotheca Sacra* (July—September 1977), 221.

21

Sexual Abuse:
The Victims
of Society

When man fell (Gen. 3), his sense of values became distorted, warped and depraved. Instead of eating to live, he lived to eat; thus gluttony arrived. Instead of trusting the Lord for his welfare, man sought to satisfy himself; thus covetousness arose.

In the sexual realm, God designed the anatomy of both the man and the woman. Their sexual activity was primarily to be enjoyed as lovers, with propagation secondary. This beautiful and enjoyable experience was designed to be spiritual as well as physical and emotional (Heb. 13:4).

But sin took its toll on sexuality as well. Child abuse, incest, rape, seduction of innocent people, homosexuality, premarital sex, nudism, venereal disease, marital abuse, prostitution and pornography are some of the results of man's sexual perversion and wicked imaginations (Rom. 1:21). The most common infectious disease (second only to the common cold) is venereal disease (gonorrhea). One of every four women will be molested by the age of eighteen. Six million wives are abused by their husbands, and 1.3 million teenage pregnancies occur each year.

The world's answer to all this is *sex education* in the public schools. But this has not helped stem the tide of immorality, for it has approached sexuality with amorality; after all, humanism holds man to be only an advanced animal. The originator of sex education for the schools was the Sex Information and Education Council of the

United States (SIECUS). This organization is riddled with humanists, evolutionists and even Communists.[1]

Tim LaHaye tells of his personal experience with sex education, using the 164-page manual, *Human Sexuality*. This manual is used to train sex education instructors. The training cost $175,000 and was financed by the Department of Health, Education and Welfare. The book advocates a field trip to a Planned Parenthood clinic without parental consent and a field trip to the local drug store so children age twelve or older can see where to purchase contraceptives without parental knowledge.[2] Planned Parenthood's concept of responsible "reproductive freedom" is amoral and fails to understand the real causes for teenage pregnancies.[3]

Fundamentalists hold these basic principles concerning human sexuality:

1. Sexuality was designed by God, and sex is wholesome, enjoyable and blessed by Him when practiced within marriage (Prov. 5:18, 19; Heb. 13:4).

2. Sexual deviation is a result of sin. Even though full forgiveness comes with regeneration, often patterns have been established which require counseling and perhaps professional help.

3. Sex should not be an obsession (1 Thess. 4:4, 5).

4. Violence for any reason is reprehensible, but sexual violence is especially detestable (Rom. 14:13, 14).

5. While the husband is head of the home, in the sexual relationship husband and wife are equal in authority and in mutual submission (1 Cor. 7:3, 4).

6. Sexual activity between husband and wife is limited by whatever pleases both and offends neither, but ends in intercourse. Sexuality is love in its fullest and finest sense.

Now let us look at some specific areas of sexual abuse.

Teenage Pregnancy

While teenage pregnancies are called "epidemic," the world's answers become more and more empty. Teens don't need contraceptives; they need morality! The 1.3 million teenage pregnancies cause great hardships on schooling, budgets, jobs and hospitals. About 50 percent of the teenage mothers choose to keep their babies; few choose to marry the father.

Parents must take some of the blame for not communicating with their children and failing to teach morality. Churches which teach the Bible are usually ignored or resented. Permissiveness breeds promiscuity! The answer is not abortion, but morality.

Other contributing factors are lewd television programs and movies. Hollywood has so glamorized sin that personal goals for teens are warped. Rock music, video rock and dancing all mold the morals of these children, who have mature bodies but a child's brain and a sinner's heart. Add to this drugs and alcohol, which break down moral standards and fire lustful passions, and, no wonder, there are casualties.

Another factor is the prevalence of pornography. Experiments in a northern university revealed that healthy, normal young men became sexually activated and their morals perverted to the point that they justified rape when they were exposed daily to one hour of pornography, which increased in intensity over an extended period of time.[4]

Fundamentalists have a responsibility to their teens. From the pulpit and in the classroom they must hear that sexual activity outside of marriage is *sin*. Churches must provide wholesome activities for teens to enjoy so they are not tempted to run with the world's crowd. When help and counseling are needed, it should be given lovingly but firmly. In some cases church discipline may be necessary.

Rape

Another unpleasant aspect of sexual abuse is rape. This crime is not really one of sex but one of violence. The rapist's motive is to establish power and hostility over women. It happens to women of all ages, all walks of life and all social status. Contrary to common opinion, women do not necessarily flirt and stimulate the criminal.

Many police departments are revising their methods and training their personnel in an effort to encourage more victims to report the crime. (Experts believe that for every case of reported rape, three to ten others are not reported.[5]) Rape crisis centers are being established to help women who have been victimized. Hospitals are beginning to train specific personnel to work with and examine rape victims. They are becoming more sensitive to a victim's needs as they collect evidence (hair, blood, semen) and treat any injuries.

They also protect the victims from venereal disease and possible pregnancy.

One of the reasons women have hesitated to report the crime of rape is the mental and emotional trauma of a court case. Rape victims have often been harassed and humiliated both by police officials and court officials. The woman must tell her story to the police, to the medical personnel, to the district attorney, then face the grand jury and perhaps a preliminary hearing, and finally the public trial. There she will face defense lawyers who try to destroy her credibility. A New York City defense attorney Morris Ploscowe, in his book *Sex and the Law*, refers to the crime of rape as "a single regrettable lapse in sexual behavior which has occasioned *no basic damage to the individual* or the community."[6] Maureen Dowd in her article "Rape: The Sexual Weapon" summarizes the traditional legal quagmire these victims have had to face:

> Through the centuries, laws continued to imply that the rape victim was somehow guilty. Women were expected to produce physical injuries proving resistance; psychological trauma was not enough. Defense lawyers were fond of using Balzac's celebrated statement on rape: "One cannot thread a needle when the needle doesn't stand still."[7]

Here is an example of a weak judge and his twisted logic:

> Last month Illinois Criminal Judge Christy Berkos gave a lenient sentence to notorious Plumber-Rapist Brad Lieberman, who, on top of prior rape convictions, pleaded guilty to five rape charges. In an interview, the judge explained his sentence: "Lieberman had done things that did hurt the women, but fortunately he did not hurt the women physically by breaking their heads or other things we see. He didn't cut their breasts off, for instance."
>
> The fact that a state judge could seem almost casual about rape shows that beneath the new surface sensitivity, many of the cultural prejudices linger.[8]

Such utter ignorance by this judge displays the kind of insensitive public official that fundamentalists cry out against. This vacuum in society ought to be corrected. No woman ought to fear the police and courts if she is violated; they should be her advocates and protectors.

One of the more brutal aspects of this unique sin is gang rape. This horrid wickedness is increasing, especially on college campuses. Often the rapists will sodomize the victim or demand oral sex. The trauma to the victim is not only immediate and devastating, but it continues.

Following a rape, a victim often finds that her father or husband does not understand. He may react with anger and make unfounded accusations. This only compounds the woman's problems. Studies indicate that suicide attempts and divorce are common among rape victims. The victims and their families are desperately in need of counseling and prayer. The shame and guilt that usually follow such an experience need to be talked about and faced in the light of Scripture.

The rapist also needs help. His aggressive and violent actions are vented toward women in general because of "a behavior problem rooted in emotional immaturity." A study of the typical rapist reveals he is young (fifteen to nineteen years of age). He is more apt to strike in summer than in winter, and he usually rapes the victim in her home. He usually comes from a poor home and was sexually abused as a child. However, rapists may be clergymen, physicians, lawyers, executives or teachers. They usually repeat their crime.[9]

The violation of women is one of the most heinous crimes against individuals as well as against society. It should be recognized for what it is. It violates a woman's body, her rights, her dignity and her integrity. She is marked and wounded physically and emotionally. She needs help and support and prayer. Fundamentalists need to reach out to these victims with compassion and understanding.

Wife Abuse

Another social evil in the category of sexual abuse is wife abuse. A marriage license should not be a permit for abuse and violence, but many homes have become battlegrounds. One-fourth of all murders occur in the home, and half of these are husband-wife killings. As high as 60 percent of all marriages include some physical violence; 20 percent of Americans surveyed approved of hitting a spouse.[10] Nearly six million women will be battered by their husbands or boyfriends. Of these, nearly four thousand will be beaten to death. The problem mainly involves women, but it is estimated that about 300,000 men are beaten by their wives.[11]

What causes a man to torment his wife? What kind of monster would strike a woman, blacken her eyes, break bones in the face, beat the breasts, kick the abdomen, or perhaps threaten with a knife or gun? One cause is immaturity on the part of the husband. His anger is similar to a young child's temper tantrum. Another cause is insecurity. This causes him to abuse the one person who sticks with him. A wife-beater may go into a rage at the thought of his wife leaving him. Clinical psychologist Dick Bathrick, who runs a program for wife-abusers, says, "The husband is trying to make her be closer to him by controlling her physically—and he doesn't realize that he's driving her away."[12] A third cause is a man's background. If he observed his mother being abused when he was a child—or if he himself was a victim of child abuse—he will often repeat this pattern in his own home.

An abused wife is caught in a solutionless situation. If she leaves her husband, she can be charged with desertion. And the care of the children, the family reputation, along with personal pride, often keep her in a violent home.

> Often a battered woman has grown up with violence and accepts it as a pitiful form of caring, or at least as something inevitable in a relationship. She may feel desperately that the world is a dangerous place and that she needs a protector, even a man who beats her.[13]

Compounding the problem of wife abuse is the failure on the part of some medical personnel and social agencies to understand the battered wife. Anne Flitcraft of Yale University's Institute for Social and Political Studies accuses doctors and social workers of being part of the battered wife syndrome. "They treat the women like they are crazy. Doctors fail to note signs of abuse, label battered women psychotic or hypochondriacal, prescribe tranquilizers and tell them to go home, and 'make a woman doubt her own sanity' by sending her to a family therapist." [14]

A unique form of wife abuse has come to light in the People's Republic of China. The Communist government has decreed that families cannot have more than two children. Pregnant mothers are *forced* to have abortions, or families are penalized. From 1971 to 1978 over 170 million abortions, tubal ligations and vasectomies were *forced* on these enslaved people. [15]

Another form of wife abuse is practiced by the husband who cheats on his wife and searches for "greener pastures." Experts estimate that one-half to three-fourths of all married men do this very thing.[16] The wives of these men are often emotionally devastated; their financial, emotional and sexual security is jeopardized; their world has been shattered.

These women need understanding and encouragement, but often fundamental churches lack programs and counseling for these victims of roaming, unfaithful husbands. God's grace is sufficient to carry a woman through such difficult days, but she needs our loving, caring support.

Fortunately, laws are being changed to help physically battered women. While legal action is not the entire solution, abused women ought to have protection. Fundamentalists repudiate violence and abuse. No wife should remain in a home where she is threatened. "God hath called us to peace" (1 Cor. 7:15). Violence is such a terrible scourge against the family. Fear and terror destroy the security and enjoyment of relationships. And violence breeds more violence. Richard Gelles, a sociologist at the University of Rhode Island, describes the grim picture of violence in the home: "The husband will beat the wife. The wife may then learn to beat the children. The bigger siblings learn it's O.K. to hit the little ones, and the family pet may be the ultimate recipient of violence."[17]

Often alcohol, unfaithfulness or other sins complicate home life. Only the gospel of Christ can change the lives of those involved. And only the grace of Jesus Christ can change the tempers and ugliness which grip so many homes.

Child Abuse

A heart-stirring report was given a few years ago about the slum children of Brazil, South America. Two million children were abandoned by their parents, and another quarter million were living in terrible poverty. Called "nobody's children," these children became social cripples, often forming bands of thieves or becoming prostitutes or other criminals.[18] Accounts of child slavery reveal 55 million children, under the age of fifteen being exploited as workers; India has 20,000; Columbia has 3 million; Hong Kong employs girls under fourteen; Morocco uses girls under thirteen.[19] Iran reported using twelve- to seventeen-year-olds in the front lines of its war against Iraq.

An even more horrible story of child abuse is unfolding here in the United States. Over one million children are runaways each year; 55,000 of these are never heard of again. An estimated 300,000 children are sexually abused each year by family members or friends, according to Martha Kendrick of the National Center on Child Abuse and Neglect in Washington, D.C.[20] Actual incest cases are estimated at 100,000 per year. The victim can be as young as three years of age, but the most common age is six or seven. Half of the incest cases begin before the child reaches puberty. The most prevalent type is between siblings and is the least destructive; the rarest, but most devastating type, is between mother and son. All strata of society are involved.[21] By the age of eighteen years, one in four girls and one in ten boys will have experienced some form of sexual abuse. Children who are abused often become abusers and/or criminals themselves. Ninety percent of the inmates at San Quentin were abused as children.

An excellent book on the problem of incest is *Kiss Daddy Goodnight* by Louise Armstrong (New York: Pocket Books, 1978). One woman which this author counseled had been abused by her father since the age of six or seven and was even preyed upon after she was married! Needless to say, deeply rooted emotional problems make normal married life difficult.

Here is a typical testimony of the results of sex abuse to a child now grown but still haunted by the memories. In a letter to Ann Landers, this woman shares the following story:

> Dear Ann Landers: I know you have helped many people. I am praying that you can help me, too. You are my only link to sanity.
>
> I am 26, married to a wonderful man, and we have a darling 3-year old son. To look at me you'd think I was the happiest person alive, but deep down I am tortured by something that happened 21 years ago. I can remember it as

though it was yesterday. My brother abused me sexually when I was 5.

I don't know how long it went on, but I recall I was in kindergarten when he started. After a while he stopped. I convinced myself that it didn't happen—that I had dreamed it, or a friend had told me it happened to her.

When I was 11, my brother tried it again. By that time I knew it was wrong and warned him to stay away from me. Everything that happened when I was 5 came back to me. I could no longer block it out.

When I was 15, I got mad at my brother for something totally unrelated and we got into a shouting match in front of my mother. I blurted out all the terrible things he had done to me when I was a child. He called me "crazy." My mother said I was lying and if she ever heard me talk like that again, she would have nothing more to do with me. I had all these conflicting emotions—anger, guilt, fear of losing my mother's love and resentment because she believed my brother and not me.

For weeks I am OK, then suddenly I remember the past and get headaches, can't sleep, and hate for my husband to touch me. I realize it isn't fair to him, so I give in. I don't like sex at all. I get nothing out of it. I know this is not normal, especially since my husband is adoring and attractive.

I can't get counseling because I would rather die than tell my husband why I am seeking help. Please hurry some advice. I am—Hanging On In Kansas.

Dear Hanging: Tell your husband you need counseling to learn why you cannot sleep and have frequent headaches. If you are lucky enough to get a competent therapist, he (or she) will help you muster the courage to tell your husband about your torturous past.

The ability to accept his loving support will strengthen your relationship and build a bridge of trust. I urge you to act on this advice at once. Look in the phone book under "mental health" or ask your physician to recommend someone.

And please stay in touch with me. I want to know how you are doing.[22]

Fundamentalists need to help the victims of abuse, and often they are not far away! Children need to know they can come and share their problems. They know when they are abused. Psychiatrist William Walter Menninger says children usually can recognize the differences between touches. "One little boy told me that with affection there is a feeling that you are being given something, but with incest he felt a sense that something was being taken away."[23]

Fundamentalists grieve over the mutilation and violation of these children. Warnings and instruction must be given to young people. The body of a believer belongs to the Lord and must not be desecrated (1 Cor. 6:19, 20).

One final comment is needed. In my opinion the worst kind of sexual abuse is when the physician, psychiatrist or pastor takes advantage of someone who has come for counseling. To seduce and to have sexual contact with a patient or person seeking help is reprehensible. (Recently a former choir girl sued seven Roman Catholic priests for $21 million because she said they seduced her.[24]) The pastor's study is sacred ground. Shame on any pastor or professional counselor who takes advantage of someone who trusts him and is seeking his help.

Should pastors who violate this sacred trust be permitted to continue in the ministry? I am convinced it is necessary to distinguish between *weakness* and *wickedness*. There can be restoration for a pastor or missionary who has fallen due to extreme circumstances and is restored with genuine repentance and humility. But there are those whose hearts are wicked. They do not show or experience repentance, and they usually lie when faced with their sin. Frequently these are habitual offenders. It is these chronic deviates whom Paul commands to be exposed before the Christian community (1 Tim. 5:20).

The church which ordained a fallen preacher should call a church council to examine the evidence for withdrawing the ordination. (Some people believe the church where his membership is held should call the council.) Only local churches have this authority, and they should prayerfully use it.

Make no mistake about it; those who continue to sin will not escape. It may be in this life their disgrace will be known, or it may be in the next (1 Tim. 5:24, 25), but God is not mocked (Gal. 6:7, 8). If a minister wrecks a local church, the Lord will ruin him (1 Cor. 3:17).

Notes:

1. Harold Lindsell, "Sex, SIECUS, and the Schools," *Christianity Today* (January 30, 1970), 11.

2. LaHaye, *The Battle for the Family*, p. 95.

3. Addie Jurs, "Planned Parenthood Advocates Permissive Sex," *Christianity Today* (September 3, 1982), 20.

4. "Woman to Woman" television program (aired March 26, 1983).

5. Andra Medea and Kathleen Thompson, "Trial Can Be as Humiliating as the Crime," *Ames Daily Tribune* (November 11, 1974), 7.

6. "Rape: The Unmentionable Crime," *Good Housekeeping* (date unknown), 194.

7. Maureen Dowd, "Rape, the Sexual Weapon," *Time* (September 5, 1983), 28.

8. Ibid., p. 29.

9. Ibid., p. 28.

10. Jane O'Reilly, "Wife Beating: The Silent Crime," *Time* (September 5, 1983).

11. Ibid.

12. Ibid., p. 26.

13. Ibid., p. 24.

14. Ibid.

15. Steven W. Mosher, "The Grim Game of Chinese Birth Control," *Houston Chronicle* (February 17, 1984).

16. Keith Pope, "Affairs Advice," *Houston Post* (February 21, 1984).

17. "Private Violence," *Time* (September 5, 1983), 18.

18. "Brazil's Wasted Generation," *Time* (September 11, 1978), 32.

19. "Child Slavery," *Time* (date unknown), 41.

20. Television news program.

21. Jessica Treadway, "Child Sexual Abuse Found Reality in All Sections of Society in U.S.," *Houston Chronicle* (November 20, 1983).

22. Ann Landers, "Brink of Insanity Produces Anger, Guilt, Fear of Losing Love," *Houston Chronicle* (March 16, 1984).

23. Holly Morris and Richard Sandza, "An Epidemic of Incest," *Newsweek* (November 30, 1981), 68.

24. " 'Aspiring Nun' Charges Priests with Seduction," *Kansas City Kansan* (February 9, 1984).

22

Suicide:
The Heartache
of Society

What makes suicide such an awesome problem is that the segment of society which is most affected is the teenager. Second only to accidents, suicide is the next leading cause of death between the ages of fifteen and twenty-four. An estimated 7,000 teenagers kill themselves annually, and as many as 400,000 attempt it![1] Every minute someone in the world ends his own life.[2] In addition to teenagers, high suicide rates are found among alcoholics, those who are depressed, Indians and Eskimos. The highest suicide rate occured in 1932 during the Great Depression. During the 1970s seventy-three suicides were committed daily.[3]

As tragic as suicide and the despair which leads up to it can be, it is compounded by the erroneous teaching of the Roman Catholic church, which condemns the suicide victim to eternal damnation and denies the victim a church burial.[4] In the Middle Ages, the corpse of a suicide victim was dragged through the streets or left unburied as a public spectacle. Even the English forefathers, such as John Bunyan, held that suicide was worse than homicide. Not until 1644, when John Donne gave some justifiable circumstances which made suicide not a hopeless disgrace, was the attitude changed. Today existential philosophy teaches that death is not to be feared, but that it is the logical goal of life. This is not in the sense of Christian hope, but rather the end of existence (like the death of an animal).

The Bible makes it clear that every person has an eternal soul;

he will live forever. He will spend eternity either with the Lord or separated from Him; but eternity is a reality. For a believer to take his own life is spiritual insanity, but he does not forfeit his eternal life in Heaven. However, suicide is a selfish, sinful, willful act of rebellion for it says, in effect, that God cannot solve the problem which led to the taking of one's own life.

Why do people attempt to take their own lives? Probably the major reason is the desire to communicate to others unhappiness or hopelessness. In reality, suicide is a selfish act, with the victim proclaiming, "I'll show them!" Two psychologists in Los Angeles compared fake and genuine suicide notes. The genuine ones were specific, with instructions to relatives. These psychologists coined the term "cry for help" as these messages were a plea for someone to notice and help. They were a final communication when all other forms had broken down.[5]

Depression is also a major cause for suicide attempts. A profound feeling of worthlessness and low self-esteem accompany depression. The depressed person has a negative view of the world, and hopelessness about the future obsesses his thinking. This makes suicide seem tempting. Crying, sleeplessness, lethargy and lack of purpose consume the depressed person. Unruly temper and wild behavior may develop. Teenagers drop out of school. Some people become heavy drinkers. For others, jobs and friends are given up. The National Center for Disease Control in Atlanta reports that one of every six severely depressed people will eventually take his own life.

Another major cause of suicide is the loss of a loved one. The death or other loss of a spouse or family member may leave a terrible vacuum and great loneliness. Serious illness and financial failure may also cause a person to feel hopeless. The fear of pain also contributes to the suicidal mind. Some types of mental illness and psychosis may also lead to suicide.

Some people commit "slow suicide"; that is, they consciously commit themselves to hard drugs or alcohol, knowing this will cause eventual death. Fast driving and dangerous actions often characterize this reckless mentality. Karl Menninger calls these types "chronic suicides."[6]

Klagsburn lists several practical suggestions on how to help in a suicidal crisis: (1) recognize the clues to suicide (threats, despair, etc.); (2) trust your own judgment; (3) tell others; (4) stay with a suicidal person; (5) listen intelligently; (6) urge professional help; (7) be supportive.[7]

One of the resultant tragedies of a suicide is the guilt of family members and friends. They are often devastated, and they need encouragement with their hurt and humiliation. They often need to relate their quest for justification or forgiveness. If the survivor is a Christian, Hebrews 4:16 can be a blessed instruction: "Let us therefore come boldly unto the throne of grace, that we may obtain mercy, and find grace to help in the time of need." Here the believer can find forgiveness if failure and guilt are his burden ("mercy"); or, if he is mystified over his loved one's suicide or does not know the cause of the suicide, he can find grace. What a blessing to the grieving, wounded heart to lay this burden at the throne of grace. The healing hand of the Lord ministers in that mysterious, inexplicable peace which only He can supply (Phil. 4: 6, 7).

Preventing suicide is a worthy ministry for fundamentalists. One way of doing this is to offer counsel to depressed persons, giving them reasons to live. (Note Paul's testimony in Philippians 1:21, "For to me to live is Christ, and to die is gain.") Only Christ can replace dullness and discouragement with new, fresh hope. When someone threatens suicide, he should be taken seriously and urged to get help, including counseling and prayer.

Second Timothy 4:6–8 is a wonderful passage to share with a troubled Christian who has given up hope. An unsaved person needs the gospel of Jesus Christ. Christ alone can provide hope (Titus 2:13) and a reason for living.

Notes:

1. Jeannye Thorton, "Behind a Surge in Suicides of Young People," *U.S. News & World Report* (June 20, 1983), 66.

2. Weldon Burge, "Suicide," *Faith for the Family* (September 1979), 1.

3. "Suicide Most Likely on Mondays during Springtime, Study Shows," *Houston Chronicle* (February 22, 1984).

4. Burge, p. 4

5. Klagsburn, *Too Young to Die*, p. 30.

6. Ibid., p. 64.

7. Ibid., p. 96.

23

Warfare and Self-Defense: The Protection of Society

As we study history, we see that warfare has played a major part in the affairs of men and nations. While the selfish motives of man are usually the cause of war, the Scriptures do bear record that God uses warfare to accomplish His purpose. Israel was to defend herself against the pagan nations which threatened her (Num. 32:5-23), and men were justified in defending their possessions from intruders (Exod. 22:2, 3).

> Be not thou envious against evil men, neither desire to be with them.
> For their heart studieth destruction, and their lips talk of mischief.
> Through wisdom is an house builded; and by understanding it is established.
> And by knowledge shall the chambers be filled with all precious and pleasant riches.
> A wise man is strong; yea, a man of knowledge increaseth strength.
> For by wise counsel thou shalt make thy war: and in multitude of counsellors there is safety (Prov. 24:1-6).

> He teached my hands to war, so that a bow of steel is broken by mine arms (Ps. 18:34).

> Blessed be the LORD my strength, which teacheth my hands to war, and my fingers to fight (Ps. 144:1).

The New Testament adds to the Old Testament principle of self-defense by stating that human government has the sacred responsibility of protecting its citizens. Thus, the Christian should support and pay for this secular authority (Rom. 13:1–7).

> Submit yourselves to every ordinance of man for the Lord's sake: whether it be to the king, as supreme;
> Or unto governors, as unto them that are sent by him for the punishment of evildoers, and for the praise of them that do well (1 Pet. 2:13, 14).

Should a Christian refuse to serve in the military of his country or refuse to defend his property? It would seem clear "for conscience sake" (Rom. 13:5) he should be involved in the use of force to control aggressive and violent men. Robert L. Moyer, former dean at Northwestern Bible School and Seminary, gave this blunt rebuke of conscientious objection:

> Can a man Scripturally be a conscientious objector? Our answer is *No*. Romans 13:5 indicates that a man is to be subject to the powers that be "not only for wrath, but also for conscience sake." There goes your conscientious objection. Obedience to rulers is not a worldly matter; it is a religious duty.[1]

Not until the Roman custom of Caesar worship did serving in the military become incompatible for Christians. There seems to be no record of Christians in the army until about A.D. 174. Then Celsus, the famous heretic, rebuked believers for not sharing the responsibility of defending the Roman Empire against the barbarian threat. But there does not seem to be much participation except for noncombatant positions. Constantine made Christianity legal and opened the army to Christians. Following Constantine, Christians were active in the military. Augustine (A.D. 400) defended just wars as being necessary, but they must have peace as their goal.[2]

Roman Catholicism justified warfare for its own ends. It taught that Luke 22:38 meant one sword was for the church and the other for secular or civil government. Its policy of the church directing civil authorities is a tragic record of brutality and savagery. The Inquisition, for example, was justified because it accomplished the pope's desires.

The leaders of the Reformation differed over warfare, some justifying the resistance of evil and others more reluctant to approve of violence in any form. Luther regretted the necessity of having to secure protection from the German princes. But he supported them when they destroyed the Turks or the Anabaptist peasants. Zwingli, the great reformer of Zurich, had no hesitation to use the civil power of the sword to achieve spiritual goals. His statue shows him holding both Bible and sword. In fact, he died on the battlefield as a chaplain-combatant. John Calvin of Geneva, while supporting civil government as needful, was reluctant to support violence. He counseled Christians to flee whenever possible, or to use non-resistance when persecuted.[3]

The European Anabaptists held different views, but they seemed to be mostly pacifists. They did not deny the civil government the responsibility of bearing the sword, but they would not take up the sword themselves. Today Brethren and Mennonite groups, the Quakers and liberal churches take similar positions.[4]

The logic of these early pacifists is that since the Christian is not of this world, he should not fight for this world. They use Scriptures such as Matthew 5:43, 44; Luke 9:55, 56; John 18:36; Romans 12:21; 2 Corinthians 10:4. The Christian, according to this philosophy, is only a citizen of Heaven, not of this world.

The aggressive and wicked atrocities of Adolf Hitler in the twentieth century have disturbed European pacifism, but not the American strain. The aftermath of the atomic bombs dropped on Japan was a catalyst to the pacifist movement in the United States.

The pacifist spirit today is generally much different than that of post-apostolic times or the Reformation era. It is a political motivation against the horrors of nuclear weapons and the astronomical cost of military preparation. Unfortunately, liberal theology and liberal politics do not seem to understand the worldwide threat of international communism. The reluctance to stand against this incalculable danger—not only to Christianity but to civilization—has put the free world in serious jeopardy.

One of the most knowledgeable spokesmen warning the

Western world of the real danger from Communist expansion is author Alexander Solzhenitsen, the Soviet exile. He warns, "The entire 20th century is being sucked into the vortex of atheism and self-destruction"[5] Solzhenitsen is critical of Billy Graham for his sellout to Soviet propaganda and his "deplorable statement that he had not noticed the persecution of religion in the U.S.S.R."[6]

Sidney Hook, the senior researcher at Stanford University's Hoover Institution, wrote in his book *Marxism and Beyond* this warning about pacifism: "What if the enemies of a free society are not inspired by this spirit of Christian submission? What if, interpreting pacifism and appeasement in good Leninist fashion as an expression of cultural decadence, they move to take over the remaining centers of freedom?"[7]

Two significant developments of which fundamentalists should be aware are these: (1) The Roman Catholic church in America through the decisions of its bishops has declared almost total rejection of this nation's rearmament. These clergymen have the presumption to call for the consideration of unilateral disarmament. They want a nuclear freeze on the part of the United States. The House of Representatives has voted a nonbinding resolution for this freeze.

(2) The new evangelicals in America are fast moving toward pacifism or, even worse, capitulation. One of their leading spokesmen is Ron Sider, professor at Eastern Baptist Seminary and president of the Evangelicals for Social Action. He has stated: "We would meet them [the Russians] on the shores, on our knees, praying for them, but standing together and vowing not to cooperate with any of their orders."[8] Dr. Sider proposes dismantling the United States military complex entirely and having a civilian-based defense modeled after Gandhi's concept of nonviolent noncooperation. Another pacifist is Jim Wallis of *Sojourners* periodical, which stands for stopping the arms race militarily.[9] The National Association of Evangelicals is fast moving to the left and identifying with liberal causes.[10]

The principle taught in the Scriptures is that the *strong man* is the one who resists the evil intruder. Wicked men cannot be trusted. The devil and his crowd cannot be negotiated with or bargained with. Every nation the Communists have taken over is closed to gospel missions. Believers in these countries are suffering under this satanic movement. Fundamentalists stand for the defense of freedom through wise and uncompromising leadership. Nuclear weapons are a necessary part of that defense. But it is the God of Heaven and earth that must graciously preserve the free world for gospel preaching and prophetic designs.

The consequence of any war is devastation, and a nuclear war is utter nonsense. But as John Stuart Mills said, "War is an ugly thing, but not the ugliest of things: the decayed and degraded state of moral and patriotic feeling which thinks nothing is worth a war is worse."

Notes:

1. Robert L. Moyer, "The Christian and War," *The Sword of the Lord* (July 1, 1983), 15.

2. Robert Culver, "Between War and Peace: Old Debate in a New Age," *Christianity Today* (October 24, 1980), 30–32.

3. Ibid., p. 33.

4. Ibid., p. 34.

5. "Return to God," *Time* (May 23, 1983), 57.

6. Ibid.

7. Sidney Hook, "We Must Not Give In," *Houston Chronicle* (May 16, 1983).

8. Robert Biscoe, *Fundamental News Service* (August 1983), 2.

9. Ibid.

10. Richard Pierard, "NAE's Social Awareness Grows," *Christianity Today* (April 9, 1982), 42.

V

Restatement of Biblical Position

"Nevertheless we, according to his promise, look for new heavens and a new earth, wherein dwelleth righteousness. Wherefore, beloved, seeing that ye look for such things, be diligent that ye may be found of him in peace, without spot, and blameless" (2 Peter 3:13, 14).

Conclusion

As the church faces social issues, she needs to be careful to correctly understand and properly apply these Biblical truths:

The Separation of Church and State

The believer must become involved in two sacred responsibilities. The primary responsibility is the local church, and the secondary one is citizenship. God established both the church and the state. He wants both to function in friendship but not dependence upon each other. Nor should one dominate and dictate to the other. Much of the conflict in society has been caused by one trying to control the other. Jesus said, "Render therefore unto Caesar the things which are Caesar's; and unto God the things that are God's" (Matt. 22:21).

The Dispensations of Bible History

Unless the hermeneutical principle of dispensationalism is followed, there will be confusion in understanding Bible truth. For example, Matthew 24 and 25 deal specifically with the events of the Tribulation period. To bring Messianic earthly kingdom principles into the New Testament church causes doctrinal havoc and confusion. To impose instructions given to Israel on the New Testament people of God is unfortunate. To force kingdom truth upon unsaved society is unscriptural. It is absolutely essential to hold to the doctrine of the premillennial return of Christ and the establishment of His kingdom to interpret the Bible correctly. Otherwise, the Bible student will not understand the church and its sacred mission in this age of grace. Dr. Ryrie emphasizes this vital point with this valuable commentary:

This is one of those tensions under which Christians live. They know that they cannot bring peace, righteousness, or social justice; these will be accomplished only by Christ at His second coming. At the same time they know equally well that they ought to pray for peace and practice righteousness. Realistic dispensational premillennialism acknowledges both. Christians will not win the war until He comes; yet they must fight to win battles now.[1]

The Mission of the Church

The overwhelming view of Regular Baptists is that any social ministry should be limited to *believers* in their needs.[2] The one exception which could be justified is when a social ministry gives opportunity for sharing the gospel. Some examples of this would be medical missions, city rescue missions, servicemen's centers and possibly emergency funds for certain crises such as famines or earthquakes. Great care must be maintained to prevent drifting into purely benevolent social activity because of the desperate needs of people. This is especially pertinent with medical or educational missions in primitive nations.

Theo J. W. Kunst in his article "The Kingdom of God and Social Justice" lists the priorities for Christians to follow.

> In view of these truths about present and future salvation, the future messianic kingdom, and present-day responsibilities, Christians have several priorities to which they should give their attention. Their first priority is their relationship with the Lord. . . . A Christian's second priority is his marriage. . . . The third priority is a believer's relationship to his local church. . . . A fourth priority for believers is in citizenship. They should seek to witness for Christ in school, business, their professions, etc. Within the political framework of his country, each Christian should try to express biblical principles in order to further the interests of everyone.
>
> Each Christian should obey the authorities (whether chosen by him or not), as institutions established by God, knowing that God is to be obeyed in the first place.[3]

A different approach to priorities is given by Franky Schaeffer in his book *A Time for Anger*. Franky is the son of the famed Francis Schaeffer and is an author, film director and artist. He makes his plea for political action with this logic:

> Of all people, Christians should not be the friend of the status quo, for the status quo, the reign of the devil, is what Christ came to redeem. To speak of a gospel that does not have political implications or a Bible whose laws do not apply to the modern world subverts the entire thrust of Christianity, which is to reclaim for God what has been lost through man's disobedience. To accept the idea that there is any part of life that Christianity should not affect, whether it be the family, politics, the law, the media, or the arts, is to make a tacit admission that Christianity is not true.
>
> We must act, and act now. We must dare to be human. We must dare to sacrifice in a selfish age. We must dare to be unfashionable. Dare to live, and dare to let the defenseless live.[4]

In spite of all this passion, the Bible student must have serious reservations with Schaeffer's view. Christians should indeed oppose publicly and politically causes which are immoral. But the Bible does not teach that the gospel has an application to the evils of society, but to the evil of the human heart. Christianity's truth or untruthfulness does not rest upon its changing society's morals!

To be sure, the obedient Christian should take his citizenship seriously. He should vote and should support his government in its proper function, including serving in the military. He should protest unjust and immoral issues which his government may promote. But that action is far different from attempting to "Christianize society." Only the returning Lord of Glory can establish "a new earth, wherein dwelleth righteousness" (2 Pet. 3:13). This world is heading for destruction and judgment whether or not zealous Christian leaders believe it!

What, then, should be the passion of the believer toward the Satan-controlled and contaminated society? Jude summarized the goals of the believer in his short epistle:

But you, beloved, building yourselves up on your most holy faith; praying in the Holy Spirit;

keep yourselves in the love of God, waiting anxiously for the mercy of our Lord Jesus Christ to eternal life.

And have mercy on some, who are doubting;

save others, snatching them out of the fire; and on some have mercy with fear, hating even the garment polluted by the flesh.

Now to Him who is able to keep you from stumbling, and to make you stand in the presence of His glory blameless with great joy,

to the only God our Savior, through Jesus Christ our Lord, be glory, majesty, dominion and authority, before all time and now and forever. Amen (Jude 20–23; NASB).

Here are the marching orders for Christians. Snatch individuals *from* the decadent society. Look to the only real hope and answer, the coming Christ Who will judge the quick and the dead, Who will right the wrongs in His time. America is not Israel, and preachers are not prophets. Prayer, godly living and Scriptural doctrine are the means of faithful obedience. And, bless God, *He* will keep the believer and prevent his falling into the world's evils by His sovereign power.

In his message "The Role of the Church in Social Problems," Howard Kershner gives a powerful insight with this statement:

The church must choose to depend upon and to invoke divine power which knows no limit and overcomes every obstacle or to place its faith in the feeble efforts of man. Let us hope that it will recover from its temporary obsession with man-made institutions, and quickly rise again to the spiritual level, resuming its proper function of proclaiming the gospel of Christ as the means of individual salvation— the only road to the solution of our social problems.[5]

Fundamentalism has had its weaknesses and extremists, but its philosophy of ecclesiastical separation and emphasis on the spiritual rather than a social ministry is Biblical. While society and nations change, the Scriptures do not and the real need for sinful man does not.

The apostle Paul's warning should be heard and heeded in this day of deception and confusion over social and political action.

> For many walk, of whom I often told you, and now tell you even weeping, that they are enemies of the cross of Christ,
> whose end is destruction, whose god is their appetite, and whose glory is in their shame, *who set their minds on earthly things.*
> For our citizenship is in heaven, from which also we eagerly wait for a Savior, the Lord Jesus Christ;
> who will transform the body of our humble state into conformity with the body of His glory, by the exertion of the power that He has even to subject all things to Himself (Phil. 3:18–21; NASB).

Notes:

1. Charles C. Ryrie, "Perspectives on Social Ethics, Part I," *Bibliotheca Sacra* (January—March, 1977), 43.
2. Commons, ". . . Social Concern," p. 10.
3. Theo J. W. Kunst, "The Kingdom of God and Social Justice," *Bibliotheca Sacra* (April—June 1983), 114, 115.
4. Franky Schaeffer, *A Time for Anger* (Westchester, IL: Crossway Books, 1982), p. 137.
5. Howard Kershner, "The Role of the Church in Social Problems"; unpublished sermon, n.d.

Bibliography

I. General Bibliography
Books

Anderson, John B. *Between Two Worlds: A Congressman's Choice*. Grand Rapids: Zondervan Publishing House, 1970.

Arnot, William. *The Parables of Our Lord*. Grand Rapids: Kregel Publications, 1981.

Barclay, William. *And Jesus Said: A Handbook on the Parables of Jesus*. Philadelphia: Westminster Press, 1970.

Berkhof, Louis. *Systematic Theology*. Grand Rapids: Wm. B. Eerdmans, 1946.

Blackstone, W. E. *Jesus Is Coming*. New York: Fleming H. Revell, 1908.

Boettner, Loraine. *The Millennium*. Philadelphia: Presbyterian and Reformed, 1958.

Breese, David. *Seven Men Who Rule the World from the Grave*. Oklahoma City: The Southwest Radio Church, 1980.

Bright, Bill. *Come Help Change Our World*. San Bernardino, CA: Here's Life Publishers, 1979.

Brown, D. Mackenzie. *Ultimate Concern*. New York: Harper & Row, 1965.

Brown, L. Duane. *Biblical Basis for Baptists*. North Ridgeville, OH: D & B Reproduction Service, 1983.

Bundy, Edgar C. *Collectivism in the Churches*. Wheaton, IL: The Church League of America, 1975.

Chafer, Lewis Sperry. *The Kingdom in History and Prophecy*. Chicago: Moody Press, 1943.

Clouse, Robert G. *The Cross and the Flag*. Carol Stream, IL: Creation House, 1972.

Cox, Harvey. *The Feast of Fools.* New York: Harper & Row, 1969.

Cox, Harvey. *The Secular City.* New York: Macmillian Co., 1966.

DeHaan, Richard W. *Marriage, Divorce and Remarriage.* Grand Rapids: Radio Bible Class, 1979.

DeHaan, Richard W. *The New Morality.* Grand Rapids: Radio Bible Class, 1969.

Dobbs, Zygmund. *The Great Deceit.* West Sayville, NY: Veritas Foundation, 1964.

Dobbs, Zygmund. *Keynes at Harvard.* West Sayville, NY: Probe Research, 1962.

Dollar, George W. *A History of Fundamentalism in America.* Greenville, SC: Bob Jones University Press, 1973.

Drake, Durant. *The Problems of Religion.* New York: Houghton Mifflin Co., 1916.

Duncan, Homer. *The Ecumenical Movement in the Light of the Holy Scriptures.* Lubbock, TX: Missionary Crusader, 1976.

Falwell, Jerry. *The Fundamentalist Phenomenon.* Garden City, NY: Doubleday Co., 1981.

Fosdick, Harry Emerson. *The Challenge of the Present Crisis.* New York: Association Press, 1917.

Gaebelein, Arno C. *The Seven Parables.* New York: Arno C. Gaebelein, n.d.

Habershon, Ada. *The Study of the Parables.* Grand Rapids: Kregel Publications, 1979.

Hansen, George. *To Harass Our People.* Washington, D.C.: Positive Publications, 1984.

Harkness, Georgia. *John Calvin—The Man and His Ethics.* New York: Abingdon Press, 1958.

Hatfield, Mark O. *Conflict and Conscience.* Waco, TX: Word Books, 1972.

Hayden, Robert O. and Zygmund Dobbs. *The Social Gospel—Socialist Seduction of the Scriptures.* West Sayville, NY: Zygmund Dobbs, 1973.

Howell, Leon. *Acting in Faith.* Geneva: World Council of Churches, 1983.

Jackson, Paul R. *The Doctrine and Administration of the Church.* Schaumburg, IL: Regular Baptist Press, 1980.

Jones, E. Stanley. *The Christ of the American Road*. New York: Abingdon-Cokesbury Press, n.d.

Ketcham, Donn W. *The World Hurts!* Cherry Hill, NJ: Association of Baptists for World Evangelism, 1981.

Lindsell, Harold. *The World, the Flesh, and the Devil*. Washington, D.C.: Canon Press, 1974.

Lockyer, Herbert. *All the Parables of the Bible*. Grand Rapids: Zondervan Publishing House, 1979.

Marsden, George M. *Fundamentalism and American Culture*. New York: Oxford University Press, 1980.

Mason, H. Norton. *The National Council of Churches of Christ in the U.S.A.* Victoria, TX: Trinity Episcopal Church, 1967.

Mott, Stephen Charles. *Biblical Ethics and Social Change*. New York: Oxford University Press, 1982.

Murch, James DeForrest, et al. *The Coming World Church*. Lincoln, NE: Good News Broadcasting Assn., 1963.

Nash, Ronald H. *The New Evangelicalism*. Grand Rapids: Zondervan Publishing House, 1963.

Noll, Mark A., et al. *Eerdmans' Handbook to Christianity in America*. Grand Rapids: Wm. B. Eerdmans, 1983.

Nuttall, Clayton L. *The Conflict: The Separation of Church and State*. Schaumburg, IL: Regular Baptist Press, 1980.

Patton, William. *Bible Wines or Laws of Fermentation and Wines of the Ancients.* Oklahoma City: Sane Press, 1975.

Pentecost, J. Dwight. *Things to Come*. Findlay, OH: Dunham Publishing Co., 1958.

Pickering, Ernest D. *The Fruit of Compromise: The New and Young Evangelicals*. Clarks Summit, PA: Baptist Bible College of Pennsylvania, n.d.

Pickering, Ernest D. "Our Social Responsibilities," *Vital Issues of the Hour, No. 2, Adult Instructor*. Schaumburg, IL: Regular Baptist Press, 1976.

Pink, A. W. *The Prophetic Parables of Matthew Thirteen*. Covington, KY: Kentucky Bible Depot, 1946.

Quebedeaux, Richard. *The Worldly Evangelicals*. New York: Harper & Row, 1978.

Quebedeaux, Richard. *The Young Evangelicals*. New York: Harper & Row, 1974.

Schaeffer, Francis A. *The Church at the End of the 20th Century*. Downers Grove, IL: InterVarsity Press, 1971.

Secrest, Charles. *Those Red Bears—in Clergy Collars*. Tulsa, OK: Christian Crusade Publications, 1973.

Sine, Tom. *The Mustard Seed Conspiracy*. Waco, TX: Word Books, 1981.

Stowell, Joseph M. *The Liberal and the Fundamentalist*. Des Plaines, IL: Living Reality, n.d.

Strong, Augustus Hopkins. *Systematic Theology*. Philadelphia: Judson Press, 1907.

Trench, Richard Chenevix. *Notes on the Parables of Our Lord*. New York: D. Appleton & Co., 1853.

Van Dyke, Henry. *The Gospel for a World of Sin*. New York: Macmillan, 1899.

Van Gorder, Paul R. *Parables That Make a Difference*. Grand Rapids: Radio Bible Class, 1974.

Van Gorder, Paul R. *Parables That Tell Secrets*. Grand Rapids: Radio Bible Class, 1974.

Verduin, Leonard. *The Anatomy of a Hybrid*. Grand Rapids: Wm. B. Eerdmans, 1976.

Webber, Robert E. *The Secular Saint*. Grand Rapids: Zondervan Publishing House, 1981.

West, Nathaniel. *The Thousand Years in Both Testaments*. Fincastle, VA: Scripture Truth Book Co., n.d.

Williams, Colin. *Faith in a Secular Age*. New York: Harper & Row, 1966.

Williams, Julian. *The World Council of Churches: Architects of a One-World Church*. Tulsa, OK: Christian Crusade Publications, 1973.

Wurmbrand, Richard. *Was Marx a Satanist?* Glendale, CA: Diane Books, 1977.

Periodicals

Alexander, John F. "The Making of a Young Evangelical . . . or How I Became a Legalist," *The Other Side* (March—April 1975), 2–4.

Archer, Glenn L. "The Church-State Wall," *Christianity Today* (May 10, 1974), 6–12.

Beck, M. N. "The Bed Undefiled," *Christianity Today* (October 10, 1975), 4–6.

"The Chicago Call: An Appeal to Evangelicals," *Christianity Today* (June 17, 1977), 28, 29.

"Children—The Battering Parent," *Time* (November 7, 1969), 77–80.

Chilton, David. "Productive Christians in an Age of Guilt Manipulators," *The Christian Alternative* (October 1982).

Colson, Charles. "Taking a Stand When Law and Justice Conflict," *Christianity Today* (February 4, 1983), 40, 41.

"A Conversation with Young Evangelicals," *Post-American* (January 1975), 6–13.

Ditty, William. "The Mission of the Church," *Keystone Baptist* (January 1984), 1.

Dobson, Ed and Ed Hindson. "A Critical Self-Evaluation of Fundamentalism," *Fundamentalist Journal* (March 1983), 12, 13.

Dobson, Ed and Ed Hindson. "Doctrinal Differences: Do They Matter?" *Fundamentalist Journal* (April 1983), 12–14.

Dobson, Ed and Ed Hindson. "The Church in the World and against the World," *Fundamentalist Journal* (July/August 1983), 10, 11.

Dobson, Ed and Ed Hindson. "Who Are the 'Real' Pseudo-Fundamentalists?" *Fundamentalist Journal* (June 1983), 10, 11.

Doe, Jane. "I Had an Affair," *Ladies' Home Journal* (April 1984), 18–20.

"Evangelicals Study the Link Between Social Action and Gospel," *Christianity Today* (August 6, 1982), 54–56.

Forbes, W. Merwin. "Review Article," *Grace Theological Journal* (Fall 1983), 303–309.

"Fundamentalism and Fundamentalism," *Focus on Missions* (February 1983).

"Fundamentalism in a Pin-Stripe Suit?" *Christianity Today* (October 6, 1978), 12, 13.

Gentry, Kenneth L., Jr. "Bible Teaching on Civil Government," *The Christian Alternative* (November 1983).

Gentry, Kenneth L., Jr. "Bible Teaching on Civil Government, Part II," *The Christian Alternative* (December 1983), 2.

Gest, Ted. "Are Good Samaritans a Vanishing Breed?" *U. S. News & World Report* (November 14, 1983), 56–58.

Gest, Ted, et al. "When Church and State Collide," *U. S. News & World Report* (March 5, 1984), 42–46.

Haldeman, I. M. "The Mission of the Church in the World," *The Biblical Evangelist* (September 3, 1982), 8.

Hamilton, Alan H. "The Social Gospel," *Bibliotheca Sacra* (April—June 1950), 211–221.

Hamilton, Alan H. "The Social Gospel, Part II," *Bibliotheca Sacra* (July—September 1951), 310–314.

Hamilton, Alan H. "The Social Gospel, Part III," *Bibliotheca Sacra* (October—December 1951), 466–476.

Hamilton, Alan H. "The Social Gospel, Part IV," *Bibliotheca Sacra* (July—September 1952), 271–280.

Hargis, Billy James. "What Is the 'Social Gospel'?" *The Weekly Crusader* (March 14, 1969).

Henry, Carl F. H. "Martyn Lloyd-Jones: From Buckingham to Westminster," *Christianity Today* (February 8, 1980), 27–34.

Henry, Carl F. H. "The Concerns and Considerations of Carl F. H. Henry," *Christianity Today* (March 13, 1981), 18–23.

Hesselgrave, David J. "Tomorrow's Missionaries: To Whose Drumbeat Will They March?" *Christianity Today* (July 18, 1980), 24–27.

Hundley, Ray. "The Dangers of Liberation Theology," *Focus on Missions* (February 1982), 1.

Jay, William. "Christians Not of the World," *The Biblical Evangelist* (December 9, 1983).

Jones, George E. "Are Lawyers, Courts, Big Government Dulling America's Moral Sense?" *U. S. News & World Report* (September 26, 1977), 83–85.

Kunst, Theo J. W. "The Kingdom of God and Social Justice" *Bibliotheca Sacra* (April—June 1983), 108–115.

Leo, John. "Some Day, I'll Cry My Eyes Out," *Time* (April 23, 1984), 72, 73.

"The Lone Ranger of American Fundamentalism," *Christianity Today* (September 4, 1981), 22–27.

Mahaffy, Francis E. "Social Justice," *The Journal of Christian Reconstruction* (Summer 1975), 28–32.

"Mainline Church Leaders Hit for 'Obscene' Political Behavior," *Christianity Today* (April 23, 1982), 42–45.

Mann, James. " 'Soft Sell' Is New Password for Churches," *U. S. News & World Report* (August 22, 1983), 32.

Marsden, George M. "Evangelical Social Concern—Dusting off the Heritage," *Christianity Today* (May 12, 1972), 8–11.

McCall, Alan. "The Certain Victory of Christ's Kingdom," *The Christian Alternative* (January 1984).

Meredith, Albert R. "Spurgeon and His Times: The Christian's Social Responsibility," *Quarterly Review* (January, February, March 1975).

Nash, C. A. "Book Review," *Bibliotheca Sacra* (January—March 1961), 81, 82.

Nash, Ronald H. "The Economics of Justice: A Conservative's View," *Christianity Today* (March 23, 1979), 24–30.

Ockenga, Harold John. "The New Reformation," *Bibliotheca Sacra* (January—March, 1948), 89–101.

Patterson, Richard D. "The Widow, the Orphan, and the Poor in the Old Testament and the Extra-Biblical Literature," *Bibliotheca Sacra* (July—September 1973), 223–234.

Peters, George W. "Current Theological Issues in World Missions," *Bibliotheca Sacra* (April—June 1978), 153–164.

Peters, George W. "An Evangelical Response to Theological Issues in Missions," *Bibliotheca Sacra* (July—September 1978), 253–262.

Pettegrew, Larry D. "Will the Real Fundamentalist Please Stand Up?" *The Central Testimony* (Fall 1982).

Pierard, Richard V. "Social Concern in Christian Missions," *Christianity Today* (June 18, 1976), 7–10.

Pierard, Richard V. "The Bedfellows of Revival and Social Concern," *Christianity Today* (April 4, 1980), 23–25.

Plueedemann, James. "Reactions: Still Another Side to 'The Other Side,' " *Christianity Today* (November 26, 1982), 29–32.

Reynolds, M. H., Jr. "The World Council of Churches—The Cup of the Lord or the Cup of Devils?" *Foundation* (1983), 16–19.

Robinson, Haddon W. "Politics and Preaching in the English Reformation," *Bibliotheca Sacra* (April—June 1965), 120–133.

Ryrie, Charles C. "Perspectives on Social Ethics, Part I," *Bibliotheca Sacra* (January—March 1977), 33–44.

Ryrie, Charles C. "Perspectives on Social Ethics, Part II," *Bibliotheca Sacra* (April—June 1977), 114–122.

Ryrie, Charles C. "Perspectives on Social Ethics, Part III," *Bibliotheca Sacra* (July—September 1977), 215–227.

Ryrie, Charles C. "Perspectives on Social Ethics, Part IV," *Bibliotheca Sacra* (October—December 1977), 314–328.

Sargent, J. A. "Astrology's Rising Star," *Christianity Today* (February 4, 1983), 40, 41.

Shoemaker, Samuel M. "The Church and Awakening Groups," *Christianity Today* (October 10, 1960), 6–15.

Sider, Ronald J. "Evangelism or Social Justice: Eliminating the Options," *Christianity Today* (October 8, 1976), 26–29.

Smith, Charles R. "Review Article," *Grace Theological Journal* (Spring 1982), 133–137.

Smith, Harold Ivan. "Sex and Singleness the Second Time Around," *Christianity Today* (May 25, 1979), 17–22.

"Social Gospel Turns Holistic," *Focus on Missions* (February 1979).

"Socialism: Trials and Errors," *Time* (March 13, 1978), 24–40.

Taylor, Clyde W. "Where Is Your Church?" *Bibliotheca Sacra* (April—June 1965), 144–157.

Thornton, Jeannye. "The Tragedy of America's Missing Children," *U. S. News & World Report* (October 24, 1983), 63, 64.

Torbet, Robert G. "Answers to Questions Raised about Baptists and Christian Unity," *Mission* (November—December 1969).

Toussaint, Stanley D. "The Introductory and Concluding Parables of Matthew Thirteen," *Bibliotheca Sacra* (October—December 1964), 351–355.

Towns, Elmer L. "Trends among Fundamentalists," *Christianity Today* (July 6, 1973), 12–19.

"U.S. Needs a 'Moral and Social Recovery,' " *U. S. News & World Report* (January 9, 1984), 59, 60.

Walvoord, John F. "The Millennial Issue in Modern Theology," *Bibliotheca Sacra* (January—March 1949), 34–47.

Walvoord, John F. "Posttribulationism Today," *Bibliotheca Sacra* (October—December 1976), 299–311.

Webster, Douglas D. "Social Action Begins in the Local Church," *Christianity Today* (October 10, 1980), 28–31.

Welch, W. Wilbert. "The Church and Its Social Ministry," *Messenger* (June 1973), 2.

Wellborn, Stanley N. "When School Kids Come Home to an Empty House," *U. S. News & World Report* (September 14, 1981), 42–47.

Weniger, G. Archer. "The Greatest Danger of the Church Today," *Blueprint* (July 26, 1977).

Whitehead, John W. "The Christian Connection," *Christianity Today* (November 12, 1982), 31–35.

Wilkes, Peter. "No Return to Eden: The Debate over Nuclear Power," *Christianity Today* (April 4, 1980), 26–29.

Williams, Russ. "Spotlight: Evangelicals for Social Action," *Evangelical Newsletter* (October 15, 1982).

Williamson, Arthur P. "The Great Commission or the Great Commandment?" *Christianity Today* (November 26, 1982), 33–35.

Witmer, John A. "Christian Social Responsibility," *Bibliotheca Sacra* (July—September 1953), 217.

Witmer, John A. "Periodical Reviews," *Bibliotheca Sacra* (October—December 1974), 358, 359.

Witmer, John A. "Periodical Reviews," *Bibliotheca Sacra* (October—December 1975), 358, 359.

Witmer, John A. "Periodical Reviews," *Bibliotheca Sacra* (April—June 1976), 165, 166.

Witmer, John A. "Periodical Reviews," *Bibliotheca Sacra* (July—September 1982), 267.

Yamauchi, Edwin M. "How the Early Church Responded to Social Problems," *Christianity Today* (November 24, 1972), 6–8.

Newspapers

Dean, Ralph C. "A U. S. Trend to Socialism?" *Des Moines Register* (April 26, 1971).

Harper, Timothy. "U. S. Rape Laws Altered Greatly in Last 10 Years," *Houston Chronicle* (April 29, 1984).

Knutson, Lawrence L. "A Horse Trade," *Houston Chronicle* (November 19, 1983).

Loss, Charles R. "We Deny Christ When We Ignore Human Need," *Grit* (January 24, 1982).

Other Sources

Ashbrook, William E. "The New Neutralism." Columbus, OH: Calvary Bible Church, 1966.

Augsburger, Bryce. "The Cultural Mandate." April 1980.

Bunzel, Claude. "The Effects of the Social Gospel." Pasadena, CA: Twentieth Century Evangelism, n.d.

Commons, William Tracy. "What Are We Doing in Social Concern?" Informissions, 1976.

"Focus on Justice." Grand Rapids: Evangelicals for Social Action.

Frierson, Vicki and Ruthanne Garlock. "Christians Be Watchful." Dallas: Texas Eagle Forum, 1978.

Harrell, Billy. "Evangelical Relief and Development—Making Sure the Cup of Cold Water Is Given in the Name of Jesus."

Hubbard, David Allen. "Mission beyond the Mission." Pasadena, CA: Fuller Theological Seminary, n.d.

Jones, Bob, III. "The Moral Majority." Greenville, SC: Bob Jones University, 1980.

Kershner, Howard E. "The Role of the Church in Social Problems."

"A Manifesto—The Question of Religious Freedom and National Prosperity." Valley Forge, PA: The American Council of Churches, 1982.

Marshall, David. "Social Ministries—Are They Valid?" Kokomo, IN: Evangelical Baptist Missions, n.d.

Morikawa, Jitsuo. "Toward a Dialogue on Evangelism." Valley Forge, PA: American Baptist Home Mission Society, n.d.

Mott, Stephen. "Implementing Social Ministry."

"Nightline" Transcript (December 23, 1982).

Norris, David. "Christian Citizenship and America's Political Structure." Broomfield, CO: Denver Baptist Bible College, n.d.

Norris, David. "Separation of Church and State." Ames, IA: Heartland Press, n.d.

Reymonds, M. H. "An Ecumenical Tower of Babel." Los Osos, CA: Fundamental Evangelistic Association, n.d.

Sider, Ronald. "Seeds of Change Sprout in Fresno." Grand Rapids: Evangelicals for Social Action, 1982.

Van Impe, Jack. "A Call for Revival within Fundamentalism."

Villers, T. J. "Fidelity to Our Baptist Heritage." Schaumburg, IL: General Association of Regular Baptist Churches, n.d.

Weninger, G. Archer. "The Deadly Menace of the Cultural Mandate." Speech delivered to the Fundamental Baptist Fellowship, Denver, June 14, 1973.

II. Abortion
Books

Bergel, Gary, ed. *Abortion in America*. Elyria, OH: Intercessors for America, 1980.

Lyons, Dan and Billy James Hargis. *Thou Shalt Not Kill . . . My Babies*. Tulsa: Christian Crusade Publications, 1977.

Noebel, David A. *The Slaughter of the Innocent*. Tulsa: American Christian College Press, 1973.

Price, William. *Abortion: It's Killing America*. Dallas: Bible Fellowship, n.d.

Rice, John R. *The Murder of the Helpless Unborn*. Murfreesboro, TN: Sword of the Lord Publishers, 1971.

Schaeffer, Franky. *A Time for Anger*. Westchester, IL: Crossway Books, 1982.

Newspapers and Periodicals

Bail, Paul L. "Abortion: Slaughter of the Innocents," *The Christian Contender* (January 1984), 12–14.

Barcus, Nancy B. "Thinking Straight about Abortion," *Christianity Today* (January 17, 1975), 8–11.

Cottrell, Jack W. "Abortion and the Mosaic Law," *Christianity Today* (March 16, 1973), 6–9.

Dahlquist, Anna Marie. "Then You Can Have an Abortion," *Eternity* (March 1981), 42, 43.

Elam, Mark. "In Defense of Life," *The Christian Alternative* (March 1982), 2.

"Expert Says 1,500 Saved by Abortions," *Houston Chronicle* (March 8, 1984).

Fairfax, Olga. "101 Uses for a Dead (or Live) Baby," *The Christian Alternative* (March 1984), 8–11.

Gladstone, Mark. "Evidence Sought in Deaths of Fetuses," *Los Angeles Times* (February 7, 1982).

Hinthorn, Daniel R. "When Does Human Life Begin?" *Christianity Today* (March 24, 1978), 35–37.

Koop, C. Everett. "Medical Ethics and the Stewardship of Life," *Christianity Today* (December 15, 1978), 8–14.

Mayhue, Richard. "The Abortion Atrocity," *Spire* (Summer 1981), 6, 7.

Reed, Scott, Paul Framer and Rodney Clapp. "If Not Abortion, What Then?" *Christianity Today* (May 20, 1983), 14–16.

Ward, Beatrice. "A Biblical View of Abortion," *Faith for the Family* (January 1982), 3–6.

III. Alcoholism
Books

Alcoholics Anonymous. New York: Alcoholic Anonymous World Services, Inc., 1976.

Brown, Kenneth I. *The Use of Wine in the Bible.* Published by the author.

Coudert, Jo. *The Alcoholic in Your Life.* New York: Stein and Day, 1972.

Dunn, Jerry G. *God Is for the Alcoholic.* Chicago: Moody Press, 1968.

Johnson, Vernon E. *I'll Quit Tomorrow.* New York: Harper & Row, 1973.

Maxwell, Ruth. *The Booze Battle.* New York: Ballantine Books, 1978.

Living with an Alcoholic. New York: Al-Anon Family Group Headquarters, Inc., 1976.

Patton, William. *Bible Wines or Laws of Fermentation and Wines of the Ancients.* Oklahoma City: Sane Press, n.d.

Presnall, Lewis F. *Alcoholism: The Exposed Family.* Salt Lake City: Utah Alcoholism Foundation, 1977.

Solberg, R. J. *The Dry-Drunk Syndrome.* Center City, MN: Hazelden, 1980.

Van Impe, Jack. *Alcohol: The Beloved Enemy.* Nashville: Thomas Nelson, 1980.

Periodicals and Newspapers

"Alcoholism and the Church: Are You Killing with Kindness?" *Your Church* (January/February 1981), 52–55.

"Book Says 10 Percent of Drivers Drunk during Weekends," *Houston Chronicle* (May 1982).

"Checkpoints to Catch Drunk Drivers?" *U. S. News & World Report* (July 4, 1983).

"Children of Alcoholics Found Prone to Problem," *Houston Post* (February 25, 1984).

"Chronic Drinkers Who Stay Off Booze One Year Have Good Chance of Success," *Houston Chronicle* (January 1981).

Comer, James. "Are Indians Alcoholics?" *Houston Post* (August 24, 1982).

Fitzgerald, Kathleen Whalen. "Living with Jellinek's Disease," *Newsweek* (October 17, 1983), 22.

Gallup, George H., Jr. "Fragmented Families: Alcoholism's Spreading Blight," *Christianity Today* (September 18, 1981), 27.

Geisler, Norman L. "A Christian Perspective on Wine-Drinking," *Bibliotheca Sacra* (January—March 1982), 45–56.

Hubbell, John G. "A Dynamic New Approach to the Alcoholic," *Reader's Digest* (May 1976).

John, Harrison. "The Church and Alcoholism: A Growing Involvement," *Alcohol Health and Research World* (Summer 1977).

Kane, Karen. "Drinking in America," *Houston Chronicle* (May 29, 1983).

Kearney, Paul W. "Driver Had Been Drinking," *Reader's Digest* (October 1959).

Klemesrud, Judy. "1 of 20 Children Lives with a Parent Who Is an Alcoholic, Study Indicates," *Houston Chronicle* (November 7, 1982).

Leary, Stephanie A. "The Co-Alcoholic: Hostage in the Home?" *Alcoholism* (September/October), 25–27.

Lione, Louise. "Alcohol Can Damage Unborn Baby," *Houston Post* (March 16, 1984).

"Liquor and Babies," *Time* (July 14, 1975), 36.

Maisel, Albert Q. "Alcohol and Your Brain, Some News for Social Drinkers," *Reader's Digest* (June 1970).

Noll, Mark A. "America's Battle against the Bottle," *Christianity Today* (January 19, 1979), 19–21.

"Old-fashioned Mothers Are a Vanishing Species, 10-year Study Concludes," *Houston Chronicle* (September 9, 1982).

O'Reilly, Jane. "New Insights into Alcoholism," *Time* (April 25, 1983), 88, 89.

Plymat, William N. "Why Abstinence?" *Health Education* (March/April 1975).

Pokorny, Pat. "Alcoholism: 50 Million American Lives Affected," *Sunbury Daily Item* (November 20, 1978).

Pullman, Russ. "Alcoholism: Sin or Sickness?" *Christianity Today* (September 18, 1981), 22–25.

Rubin, M. McDevitt. "Taboo on Alcohol during Pregnancy Goes Way Back," *The Pittsburgh Press* (September 21, 1983).

"Serious Drinking Problem for 70% of Enlisted Men: Army," *Des Moines Register* (September 19, 1973).

"A Sickness Too Common to Cure?" *Christianity Today* (September 18, 1981), 12–14.

Sikes, Melvin P. "A Ministry to the Alcoholic," *The Texas Journal on Alcoholism* (n.d.), 63–77.

Stein, Robert H. "Wine-Drinking in New Testament Times," *Christianity Today* (June 20, 1975), 9–11.

Stokes, Bill. "Drinking Age Should Be Uniform," *Houston Post* (October 17, 1983).

Taylor, G. Aiken, "What about the Deadliest of Them All?" *Christianity Today* (June 7, 1974), 13–17.

Thompson, Barbara R. "Alcoholism: Even the Church Is Hurting," *Christianity Today* (August 5, 1983), 25–28.

Wharton, Don. "What Two Drinks Will Do to Your Driving," *Reader's Digest* (October 1951).

Wycliff, Don. "Drinking Becoming a Major Problem on College Campus," *Houston Chronicle* (January 1, 1984).

Yahraes, Herbert, "What Happens When You Drink," *Reader's Digest* (April 1957).

Other Sources

"Al-Anon—Family Treatment Tool in Alcoholism." New York: Al-Anon Family Group Headquarters, 1971.

"Alcohol." Spencer, NY: Miracle Manor, Inc., n.d.

"Alcoholism." New York: Christopher News Notes, No. 199.

"Alcoholism—the Family Disease." New York: Al-Anon Family Group Headquarters, 1972.

Criswell, W. A. "Wine or Water." Dallas: The National Voice, n.d.

"Drinking for What?" Swainsboro, GA: Southside Baptist Church, February 15, 1981.

"Drunk Driving: A Killer We Can Stop." New York: Insurance Information Institute, 1983.

Everett, Glenn D. "You Don't Have to Drink." West Des Moines, IA: Preferred Risk Mutual Insurance Company, n.d.

"44 Questions and Answers about the A. A. Program of Recovery from Alcoholism." New York: Alcoholics Anonymous World Service, 1952.

Graham, Billy. "The Abuse of Alcohol." Minneapolis: Billy Graham Evangelistic Association, 1977.

Hammond, Robert L. "Almost All You Ever Wanted to Know about Alcoholism." Lansing, MI: AID, 1973.

Hancock, David C. "I Can't Be an Alcoholic Because . . ." Lansing, MI: Michigan Alcohol and Drug Information Foundation, 1969.

Hostetter, B. Charles. "Drinking: Distinction or Delusion?" Chicago: Moody Press, 1961.

"Intervention—The Beginning of Family Recovery." Houston: Fairlight, n.d.

"Is Alcoholism a Disease?" Independence, IA: Calvary Evangelistic Center, n.d.

Katz, Sidney. "Booze: Why You Shouldn't Drink a Drop." West Des Moines, IA: Preferred Risk Mutual Insurance Company, n.d.

Kellerman, Joseph L. "Alcoholism—A Merry-Go-Round Named Denial." New York: Al-Anon Family Group Headquarters, 1969.

Kellerman, Joseph L. "A Guide for the Family of the Alcoholic." New York: Al-Anon Family Group Headquarters, n.d.

Lightner, Candy. Correspondence. Fair Oaks, CA: Mothers Against Drunk Drivers.

"So You Are Convinced that Alcoholism Is a Disease!" Houston: Star of Hope Mission, n.d.

"So You Love an Alcoholic?" New York: Al-Anon Family Group Headquarters, n.d.

"Someone Close Drinks Too Much." Rockville, MD: National Institute on Alcohol Abuse and Alcoholism, 1974.

Sumner, Robert L. "The Blight of Booze!" Murfreesboro, TN: Sword of the Lord Publishers, 1955.

"Symptoms of Alcoholism." Austin, TX: Texas Commission on Alcoholism, n.d.

Tassell, Paul. "Three Reasons Why a Christian Should Not Be a Social Drinker." Des Moines, IA, n.d.

"13 Steps to Alcoholism." East Moline, IL: Bright Star Press, n.d.

"Understanding Ourselves and Alcoholism." New York: Al-Anon Family Group Headquarters, 1973.

Williams, Terence. "Free to Care." Center City, MN: Hazelden Foundation, 1975.

IV. Crime

Andersen, Kurt. "An Eye for an Eye," *Time* (January 24, 1983), 28–39.

Bellshaw, William G. "Capital Punishment—Crime or Command?" San Francisco Baptist Theological Seminary.

Gideon, Helen. "A Shocking Approach to Crime," *Houston Chronicle* (March 4, 1984).

Press, Aric, et al. "To Die or Not to Die," *Newsweek* (October 17, 1983), 43–73.

Ryrie, Charles C. "The Doctrine of Capital Punishment," *Bibliotheca Sacra* (July—September 1972), 211–217.

van den Haag, Ernest. "The Death Penalty," *Houston Chronicle* (October 20, 1983).

Zimring, Franklin E. "The Death Penalty," *Houston Chronicle* (October 20, 1983).

V. Divorce and Remarriage
Books

Boettner, Loraine. *Divorce*. San Francisco: San Francisco Baptist Theological Seminary, 1960.

Buswell, James Oliver. *A Systematic Theology of the Christian Religion*. Grand Rapids: Zondervan Publishing House, 1962.

Fisher-Hunter, W. *The Divorce Problem*. Waynesboro, PA: MacNeish Publishers, 1952.

Hopewell, Wm. J. *Marriage and Divorce*. Cherry Hill, NJ: Niles & Phipps Lithographers, 1976.

Laney, J. Carl. *The Divorce Myth*. Minneapolis: Bethany House, 1981.

MacArthur, John, Jr. *Jesus' Teaching on Divorce*. Panorama City, CA: Word of Grace Communications, 1983.

Murray, John. *Divorce*. Philadelphia: Presbyterian and Reformed, 1961.

Murray, John. *Principles of Conduct*. Grand Rapids: Wm. B. Eerdmans, 1978.

Petri, Darlene. *The Hurt and Healing of Divorce*. Elgin, IL: David C. Cook, 1976.

Stowell, Joseph M. *Marriage Is for Keeps*. Des Plaines, IL: Living Reality, n.d.

Vigeveno, Henk S. and Anne Claire. *Divorce and the Children*. Glendale, CA: G/L Regal Books, 1979.

Periodicals and Newspapers

Billingsley, Lloyd. "Bad News about the Effects of Divorce," *Christianity Today* (November 12, 1982), 84–86.

192 | CONFRONTING TODAY'S WORLD

Fryling, Alice. "So Many Divorces," *Eternity* (October 1980), 83–86.

Kaiser, Robert J. "A Christian Looks at Marriage and Divorce," *Pulpit Digest* (May/June 1983), 33–35.

Kinnaird, William M. "Divorce and Remarriage: Ministers in the Middle," *Christianity Today* (June 6, 1980), 24–27.

Ryrie, Charles C. "Biblical Teaching on Divorce and Remarriage," *Grace Theological Journal* (Fall 1982), 177–192.

Sifford, Darrell. "Money, Sex, Parents: Top Causes of Divorce," *Houston Post* (March 16, 1984).

Stein, Robert H. "Is It Lawful for a Man to Divorce His Wife?" *Journal of the Evangelical Theological Society* (June 1979), 115–121.

"Sun Belt Now 'Divorce Belt,' Says Professor," *Houston Chronicle* (July 22, 1983).

VI. Drugs
Books

Adair, James R. *Unhooked*. Grand Rapids: Baker Book House, 1971.

Austrian, Geoffrey. *The Truth about Drugs*. Garden City, NY: Doubleday Co., 1971.

Brenner, Joseph H. and Robert Coles and Dermot Meagher. *Drugs and Youth*. Liveright, NY: Liveright Publishing Co., 1970.

Clark, Fred G. and Richard S. Rimanoczy. *The Christian School Tackles the Root of Drub Abuse*. Buena Park, CA: California Free Enterprise Association.

Combs, Bob. *God's Turf*. Old Tappan, NJ: Fleming H. Revell, 1969.

Klagsburn, Francene. *Too Young to Die*. New York: Pocket Books, 1981.

Pedigo, Jess L. *Our Drugged Youth—America's Growing Problem*. Tulsa: Christian Crusade Publications, 1971.

Sumner, Robert L. *The Menace of Narcotics*. Brownsburg, IN: Biblical Evangelism Press, 1971.

Urshan, Nathaniel A. *The Holy Spirit or Drugs?* St. Louis: Harvestime, 1973.

Periodicals and Newspapers

Andersen, Kurt. "Crashing on Cocaine," *Time* (April 11, 1983), 22–31.

Brecher, John, et al. "Taking Drugs on the Job," *Newsweek* (August 22, 1983), 52–60.

De Borchgrave, Armand. "The Cuban Connection," *Crossfire TV* (March 23, 1984).

Dunn, Marcia. "Programs Set up to Help Nurses Fight Addiction," *Houston Chronicle* (February 19, 1984).

Erickson, Carlton K. "Advances on Alcoholism," *Houston Chronicle* (May 3, 1982).

Fost, Norman. "Let Them Take Steroids," *Houston Chronicle* (September 14, 1983).

Landers, Ann. "Drugs," *Houston Chronicle* (November 18, 1982).

Landers, Ann. "Drugs," *Houston Chronicle* (September 7, 1983).

MacDonald, Donald Ian. "Drug Use: Adolescent High Jinks" *Houston Post* (December 27, 1983).

Mann, Peggy. "Marijuana Alert—Brain and Sex Damage," *Reader's Digest* (December 1979), 5.

"Marijuana, Cancer and Deformed Babies," *University of Utah Review* (March 1973).

McCormack, Patricia. "Study Shatters Myth Concerning Age, Alcoholism," *Houston Chronicle* (June 1981).

Nelson, Tom. "Most Cocaine Entering U. S. through Texas," *Houston Post* (December 13, 1983).

Rowan, Carl T. "Cocaine Hotline—Physical, Social Impact of Drug Confirmed," *Houston Post* (August 1983).

Sanoff, Alvin P. "How Drugs Threaten to Ruin Pro Sports," *U. S. News & World Report* (September 12, 1983), 64–66.

Solomon, Neil. "Why Is Medical Marijuana Harmful?" *Houston Post* (March 27, 1984).

Squires, Sally. "Cocaine Use Is a Fact of Life on Capitol Hill," *Houston Chronicle* (January 29, 1984).

"Why People Smoke Cigarettes," *The Biblical Evangelist* (November 25, 1983), 3.

Other Sources

Linkletter, Art. "The Drug Society." Washington, D.C.: National Teen-age Republicans.

"Questions and Answers—Barbituates, Amphetamines, LSD, Marijuana, Narcotics." Albany, NY: Narcotic Addiction Control Commission.

"Smoking." Harrisburg, PA: Capital Blue Cross, Pennsylvania Blue Shield.

Van Impe, Jack. "Does the Bible Say Anything about Drugs and Drug Addiction?" Sayre, PA: Bible Lightouse Press, 1971.

VII. Euthanasia

Bohlin, Ray. "Sociobiology: Cloned from the Gene Cult," *Christianity Today* (January 23, 1981), 16–19.

Forbes, W. Merwin. "Euthanasia," *Spire* (Summer 1981), 8, 9.

Tifft, Susan. "Debate on the Boundary of Life," *Time* (April 11, 1983), 68–70.

VIII. Femininity vs. Feminism

Alsdurf, Phyllis E. "Evangelical Feminists: Ministry Is the Issue," *Christianity Today* (July 21, 1978), 46, 47.

Buckley, Jack. "Paul, Women and the Church," *Eternity* (December 1980), 30–35.

Dayton, Donald W. and Lucille Sider. "Women as Preachers: Evangelical Precedents," *Christianity Today* (May 23, 1975), 4–7.

DeHaan, Richard W. *Male, Female, and Unisex.* Grand Rapids: Radio Bible Class, 1976.

Gangel, Kenneth O. "Biblical Feminism and Church Leadership," *Bibliotheca Sacra* (January—March 1983), 55–63.

Gest, Ted. "Battle of the Sexes over Comparable Worth," *U. S. News & World Report* (February 20, 1984), 73, 74.

House, H. Wayne. "Paul, Women, and Contemporary Evangelical Feminism," *Bibliotheca Sacra* (January—March 1979), 40–53.

Knight, George W., III. "Male and Female Related He Them," *Christianity Today* (October 9, 1976), 13–19.

LaHaye, Tim. *The Battle for the Family*. Old Tappan, NJ: Fleming H. Revell, 1982.

Norwood, James. "Women's 'Lib' or Liberation? Is It the Bible Way?"

Rapoport, Daniel. "ERA's Fatal Flaw," *Houston Chronicle* (December 1, 1983).

Scanzoni, John. "Assertiveness for Christian Women," *Christianity Today* (June 4, 1976), 16–18.

Scanzoni, Letha. "The Feminists and the Bible," *Christianity Today* (February 2, 1973), 10–15.

Schmidt, Ruth A. "Second-Class Citizenship in the Kingdom of God," *Christianity Today* (January 1, 1971), 13, 14.

Stouffer, Austin H. "The Ordination of Women: YES," *Christianity Today* (February 20, 1981), 12–15.

Tischler, Nancy M. "Suffer the Little Children," *Christianity Today* (May 9, 1975), 4–6.

Will, George F. "Many Questions and Few Answers about ERA," *Houston Chronicle* (June 1983).

Witmer, John A. "Periodical Reviews," *Bibliotheca Sacra* (July—September 1976), 255, 256.

IX. Gambling

Cosma, David J. "Gambling: The Odds are Against It for Christians—Here's Why!" *The Biblical Evangelist* (February 17, 1984), 1, 7, 8.

Dowd, William. "Compulsive Gambling Almost Cost Him His Life," *The Evening Press* (September 25, 1970).

Engelhard, Jack. "The Gambling Compulsion," *The Philadelphia Inquirer* (September 26, 1976), 12–15.

Frank, Stanley. "Gamblers Anonymous," *Houston Post* (May 23, 1962).

"Gambling," *At Calvary* (July 28, 1974), 1.

Hansen, John P. "What's Good about Gambling? Nothing!" *Christian Contender* (January 1984), 16, 17.

Mann, James. "Gambling Rage—Out of Control?" *U. S. News & World Report* (May 30, 1983), 28–30.

McKenna, David L. "Gambling: Parasite on Public Morals," *Christianity Today* (June 8, 1973), 4–6.

X. Genetic Engineering

Abbott, John P. "Biotechnology," *Shell News* (January 1984), 12–17.

Angus, Fay. "The Promise and Perils of Genetic Meddling," *Christianity Today* (May 8, 1981), 26–29.

Bagne, Paul. "High-Tech Babies," *Houston Post* (October 24, 1983).

Boffey, Philip M. "Vatican Collaborates with Scientists on Exploring Life's Questions," *Houston Chronicle* (November 26, 1983).

Boffey, Philip M. "Will Gene Splicing Be Worth the Risks?" *Houston Chronicle* (February 19, 1984).

"China Quietly Starts Forced Sterilization for 2-Child Couples," *Houston Chronicle* (May 29, 1983).

Chisolm, Elise T. "Putting Value on Human Life Worries Some," *Houston Chronicle* (February 24, 1984).

Cooke, Robert. "Choosing the Sex of Children May Become Possible," *Houston Chronicle* (May 29, 1983).

Dahlby, Tracy. "Japan Reportedly Used Human Guinea Pigs in War 'Experiments,'" *Houston Chronicle* (May 29, 1983).

Gardner, Eldon John. "Genetic Engineering," *Facing the Issues* (n.d.).

Hamilton, Michael P. *The New Genetics and the Future of Man.* Grand Rapids: Wm. B. Eerdmans, 1971.

Henry, Carl F. H. "Human Engineering," *Christianity Today* (September 12, 1975), 48–53.

"John Paul II Warns Genetic Scientists," *Houston Chronicle* (February 25, 1984).

Long, Karen P. "Genetic Techinque Would Let Parents Choose Child's Sex," *Houston Chronicle* (October 29, 1983).

Pierce, Henry. "Are Human Beings More Than the Chemicals They Are Made Of?" *Post-Gazette* (May 3, 1983).

"Religious Leaders Ask Federal Ban on Gene Engineering," *Houston Chronicle.*

Schmeck, Harold M., Jr. "No Clear Fraud Evidence Found in Clone Research," *Houston Chronicle* (February 26, 1984).

Schimmel, Paul. "Genetic Engineering: Blessing or Curse?" *Christianity Today* (June 2, 1978), 15, 16.

Schrage, Michael. "Religionists vs. Scientists," *Houston Chronicle* (June 26, 1983).

Smith, Charles R. "The Manipulation of Human Reproduction," *Spire* (Summer 1981), 4, 5.

Stone, Elizabeth. " 'Deformity' Called One of the Most Common Disorders of Mankind," *Houston Chronicle* (September 5, 1983).

"Test-tube Fertilization Criticized by Vatican as Immoral Practice," *Houston Chronicle* (August 1982).

"Test-tube Fertilization Might Be More Effective than Nature, Doctors Say," *Houston Chronicle* (September 8, 1983).

Trausch, Susan. "Tomorrow, and How Today's Congress Should Deal with It," *Houston Chronicle*.

Tutt, Bob. "Gene Splicing Stirs Debate That May Change Science, Humanity," *Houston Chronicle* (July 31, 1983).

Tveten, John. "Genetic Factors Affect Wildlife Survival," *Houston Chronicle* (February 15, 1984).

XI. Homosexuality
Books and Pamphlets

Bergler, Edmund. *Homosexuality: Disease or Way of Life?* New York: Hill and Wang, 1957.

Bowman, Karl M. and Bernice Engle. *The Problem of Homosexuality.* New York: American Social Hygiene Association, 1953.

Griffiths, David. Correspondence from Light Ministries, Inc., Houston.

"His New Children," Houston: Light Ministries, Inc., 1980.

Jones, H. Kimball. *Toward a Christian Understanding of the Homosexual.* New York: Association Press, 1966.

Narramore, Clyde M. *The Psychosexual Development of Children.* Rosemead, CA: The Narramore Christian Foundation, 1984.

Reuben, David. *Everything You Always Wanted to Know about Sex.* New York: Bantam Books, 1971.

Periodicals and Newspapers

Anderson, David E. "Leaders of National Council of Churches Want to 'Delay' Decision on Admission of Gays," *Houston Post* (November 26, 1983).

"Anglican Report OKs Homosexual Priests," *Houston Chronicle* (October 19, 1979).

Barshaw, Fred. "The Truth about Homosexuality, Part 2," *Fulfilling the Family* (March 1984).

Batteau, John M. "Sexual Differences: A Cultural Convention?" *Christianity Today* (July 8, 1977), 8–13.

Bockmuhl, Klaus. "Homosexuality in Biblical Perspective," *Christianity Today* (February 16, 1973), 12–18.

Brody, Jane. "A New Look at Homosexuality," *Woman's Day* (May 1972), 32, 140–142.

Cohn, Victor. "Rule Homosexuality not a 'Disorder,' " *Washington Post*.

Cornell, George W. " 'Gay' Pastors: Ecclesiastical Skyrockets," *Sunbury Daily Item* (May 17, 1978).

"Court Allows Man to Adopt Male Lover," *Christian Beacon* (July 15, 1982).

"Drop Homosexuality from List of Mental Illnesses," *Houston Chronicle*.

"Excommunicate Unrepentant Homosexuals and Lesbians," *The Christian News* (September 5, 1983).

Gallup, George. "Back Rights for Homosexuals," *Sunbury Daily Item*.

Grauley, John E. "Should We Change Our View of Homosexuality?" *Biblical Bulletin* (March 1978).

"Group Sex Therapy," *Time* (April 1, 1974), 45.

"The Homosexual in America," *Time* (January 21, 1966), 40, 41.

"The Homosexual: Newly Visible, Newly Understood," *Time* (October 31, 1969), 56–66.

"Homosexual Ordination: Bishops Feel the Flak," *Christianity Today* (March 4, 1977), 51, 52.

"Homosexuality: Biblical Guidance through a Moral Morass," *Christianity Today* (April 18, 1980), 12, 13.

Hoogendoorn, Case. "Gay Rights and Wrongs," *Eternity* (June 1981), 19, 42, 43.

Jenks, Philip E. "American Life Style," *The American Baptist* (May 1973), 34–37.

Johnston, Robert K. "Homosexuality and the Church," *Christianity Today* (July 20, 1979), 28–30.

Kantzer, Kenneth S. "Homosexuals in the Church," *Christianity Today* (April 22, 1983), 8, 9.

Kastelic, James. "Gays Find Salvation through Exodus," *Las Vegas Review-Journal* (June 27, 1981).

Landers, Ann. "Gays Don't Happen Overnight," *Houston Chronicle* (July 31, 1978).

Leo, John. "Homosexuality: Tolerance vs. Approval," *Time* (January 8, 1979), 48–51.

Lindsell, Harold. "Homosexuals and the Church," *Christianity Today* (September 28, 1973), 8–12.

Loyd, Linda. "Homosexuals at Home in Philadelphia Church," *Houston Post* (May 31, 1980).

M., I. "Metropolitan Community Church: Deception Discovered," *Christianity Today* (April 26, 1974), 13, 14.

Mann, James. "An AIDS Scare Hits Nation's Blood Supply," *U.S. News & World Report* (July 25, 1983), 71, 72.

McIntire, Carl. "Homosexuals in the Church, Major Issue for All Christians," *Christian Beacon* (July 8, 1982), 1.

Minnery, Tom. "Homosexuals Can Change," *Christianity Today* (February 6, 1981), 36–41.

"National Council of Churches Gives 'Polite No' to Mostly Gay Church," *Houston Chronicle* (November 10, 1983).

"A New Kinsey Report," *Time* (July 17, 1978), 53.

Scanzoni, Letha. "On Friendship and Homosexuality," *Christianity Today* (September 27, 1974), 11–16.

Sifford, Darrell. "Disclosure of Homosexuality Can Be Traumatic to All Concerned," *Houston Post* (November 22, 1983).

Sims, Bennett, J. "Sex and Homosexuality," *Christianity Today* (February 24, 1978), 23–30.

Ukleja, P. Michael. "Homosexuality in the New Testament," *Bibliotheca Sacra* (October—December 1983), 350–358.

Ukleja, P. Michael. "Homosexuality and the Old Testament," *Bibliotheca Sacra* (July—September 1983), 259–266.

XII. Hunger

"Africa Needs Food Aid 'Without Delay,' U.N. Says," *Houston Post* (November 8, 1983).

Bell, L. Nelson. "The Church and Poverty," *Christianity Today* (March 27, 1970), 27.

"Census Report Airs Statistics on Poor in U.S.," *Houston Post* (August 19, 1982).

Foster, Richard J. *Freedom of Simplicity*. San Francisco: Harper & Row.

Frykenberg, Robert E. "World Hunger: Food Is Not the Answer," *Christianity Today* (December 11, 1981), 36–39.

Henderson, Robert T. "Ministering to the Poor: Our Embarrassment of Riches," *Christianity Today* (August 8, 1980), 16–18.

Hillgren, Sonja. "Hunger in the U.S.—Anti-poverty Activists Planning to Issue New Report," *Houston Chronicle* (September 11, 1983).

"Hunger Strikes Children of Poor Families across Nation," *Houston Post* (November 10, 1983).

Khalid, S. M. " 'America Responds' to Hungry, Dying," *U.S.A. Today* (January 31, 1984).

Kuhn, Harold B. "The Evangelical's Duty to the Latin American Poor," *Christianity Today* (February 4, 1977), 67, 68.

Landrey, Paul. "Poor in America," *World Vision* (November 1983), 8, 9.

Mooneyham, W. Stanley. "Ministering to the Hunger Belt," *Christianity Today* (January 3, 1975), 6–11.

Olson, David. "Christians in a Hungry World," *Christianity Today* (March 10, 1978), 14–18.

"One Million Facing Famine Because of Long Draught," *Houston Chronicle* (February 3, 1983).

"Poverty Grips More Americans," *Houston Post* (February 24, 1984).

"Poverty Reported Increasing," *Houston Chronicle* (March 11, 1984).

Sider, Ronald J. "Cautions against Ecclesiastical Elegance," *Christianity Today* (August 17, 1979), 15–19.

Simon, Arthur. "Hunger: Twenty Easy Questions, No Easy Answers," *Christianity Today* (July 16, 1976), 19–22.

Singer, David. "The Crystal Cathedral: Reflections of Schuller's Theology," *Christianity Today* (August 8, 1980), 28, 29.

Sundquist, Dawn. "How Do You Deal with a Problem as Vast as World Hunger?" *World Relief* (Winter 1982).

"Starvation, Disease Victimizing Children," *Houston Chronicle* (December 17, 1982).

Wang, Bee-lan. "World Hunger: Starve It or Feed It?" *Christianity Today* (September 5, 1980), 17–20.

Witmer, John A. "Periodical Reviews," *Bibliotheca Sacra* (July—September 1981), 267, 268.

XIII. Sexual Abuse
Books

Armstrong, Louise. *Kiss Daddy Goodnight*. New York: Pocket Books, 1978.

Courtney, Phoebe. *The Sex Education Racket*. New Orleans: Free Men Speak, Inc., 1969.

Pedigo, Jess L. *X-Rated Movies—Hollywood's Scheme to Corrupt America*. Tulsa: Christian Crusade Publications, 1970.

Periodicals and Newspapers

Alexander, Shana. "A Simple Question of Rape," *Newsweek* (October 28, 1974), 110.

" 'Aspiring Nun' Charges Priests with Seduction," *Kansas City Kansan* (February 9, 1984).

Blampied, Phil. "In Massachusetts: A Hot Line to Tragedy," *Time* (November 6, 1978), 6, 13.

"Brazil's Wasted Generation," *Time* (September 11, 1978), 32, 40.

Brown, Harold O. J. "Abortion and Child Abuse," *Christianity Today* (October 7, 1977), 34.

Brownmiller, Susan. "Do You Believe the Myths about Rape?" *Family Circle* (October 1975), 38–42.

Brothers, Joyce. "How Should Women Resist Rape?" *Houston Post* (November 14, 1983).

Brothers, Joyce. "What Kind of Person Would Commit the Type of Sex Crime that Makes Headlines?" *Houston Post* (May 6, 1979).

Cook, Louise. "Sex Abuse Hotline Gets Help to Scared Children," *Sunbury Daily Item*.

Dart, John. "Survey: 40 Percent of Unmarried Evangelical Christians Have Had Premarital Intercourse," *Houston Chronicle* (November 26, 1983).

Douglas, Jack. "County Jail Rapes Not Preventable, Supervisor Says," *Houston Post* (April 17, 1984).

Douglas, Jack and John Whitmire. "Jail Rapes Less Frequent Elsewhere," *Houston Post* (March 21, 1984).

Dowd, Maureen. "Rape, the Sexual Weapon," *Time* (September 5, 1983), 27–29.

Drummond, Roscoe. "Rape Most Neglected Crime," *Sunbury Daily Item* (November 27, 1975).

Elliot, Janet. "Police Want Fewer Hospitals Treating Rape Victims," *Houston Post* (March 1984).

Elliot, Janet and Susan Parker. "Rape Victims Get Little Aid at 35 Hospitals," *Houston Post* (March 1984).

"Homosexual Rape Said Routine Part of Prison," *Binghamton Press* (March 3, 1969).

Hunt, Morton. "Teenagers and Sex," *Family Circle* (January 9, 1978), 153, 154.

Jurs, Addie. "Planned Parenthood Advocates Permissive Sex," *Christianity Today* (September 3, 1982), 16–21.

Kobler, John. "I Don't Know Why I Did It," *The Saturday Evening Post* (date unknown), 23–29, 42–53.

Landers, Ann. "Brink of Insanity Produces Anger, Guilt, Fear of Losing Love," *Houston Chronicle* (March 16, 1984).

Landers, Ann. "Society Needs To Spend Time Protecting Children from Abuse," *Houston Chronicle*.

Landers, Ann. "Teen Sex Woes," *Houston Chronicle* (December 20, 1983).

Landers, Ann. "We Must Warn Children," *Houston Chronicle* (February 3, 1984).

Latimer, Sandra L. "Teen-age Pregnancies," *Houston Chronicle* (September 1, 1981).

Lindsell, Harold. "Sex, SIECUS, and the Schools," *Christianity Today* (January 30, 1970), 10–13.

Magnuson, Ed. "Child Abuse: The Ultimate Betrayal," *Time* (September 5, 1983), 20–22.

Marks, Judi. "Victims Speak Out," *Teen* (February 1980), 26, 31, 96.

McCormack, Patricia. "Sexual Activity Can Be Hazardous to Teens' Health, Educator Warns," *Houston Chronicle* (October 30, 1983).

McIntosh, Barbara. "Children with Children," *Houston Post* (April 2, 1979).

Medea, Andra and Kathleen Thompson. "Trial Can Be as Humiliating as the Crime," *Ames Daily Tribune* (November 11, 1974), 7.

Mikulski, Barbara A. "Violence Begins at Home," *Sunbury Daily Item* (October 30, 1978).

Morris, Holly and Richard Sandza. "An Epidemic of Incest," *Newsweek* (November 30, 1981), 68.

Mosher, Steven W. "The Grim Game of Chinese Birth Control," *Houston Chronicle* (February 17, 1984).

O'Reilly, Jane. "Wife Beating: The Silent Crime," *Time* (September 5, 1983), 23–26.

Pope, Keith. "Affairs Advice," *Houston Post* (February 21, 1984).

"Private Violence," *Time* (September 5, 1983), 18.

Puma, Judi. "Teenage Pregnancy Epidemic Expands," *The Alief Advocate*.

Pyle, Hugh. "Teenage Sex! What Can Christian Parents Do?" *The Sword of the Lord* (October 3, 1980).

"Rape: The Unmentionable Crime," *Good Housekeeping* (date unknown), 105, 188–196.

Schultz, Gladys Denny. "Society and the Sex Criminal," *Reader's Digest* (November 1965), 139–146.

"30 Percent Dropout Rate Is Reported for Pregnant Teens," *Houston Chronicle* (June 16, 1981).

Treadway, Jessica. "Child Sexual Abuse Found Reality in All Sections of Society in U.S.," *Houston Chronicle* (November 20, 1983).

Varro, Barbara. "Aftermath of Rape," *Houston Chronicle* (September 24, 1979).

XIV. Suicide

" 'Blue Monday' Brings Suicide," *The Tampa Tribune* (January 17, 1984).

Burge, Weldon. "Suicide," *Faith for the Family* (September 1979), 1–4.

Feldman, Claudia. "Beyond the Statistics: Why Teens Try Suicide," *Houston Chronicle* (March 25, 1984).

Kenyan, Karen. "A Survivor's Notes," *Newsweek* (April 30, 1979), 17.

Klagsburn, Francene. "Teenage Suicide." *Family Circle* (April 5, 1977), 44, 156–160.

McFeatters, Ann. "Collecting Insurance Tough for Suicide Victims' Kin," *Houston Chronicle* (November 24, 1983).

O'Donnell, Walter E. "The Will to Live," *Woman's Day* (June 28, 1977), 50, 52, 128.

"Suicide Most Likely on Mondays during Springtime, Study Shows," *Houston Chronicle* (February 22, 1984).

"Suicide Rate among Eskimos Is Alarming," *Houston Post* (February 15, 1984).

Thornton, Jeannye. "Behind a Surge in Suicides of Young People," *U. S. News & World Report* (June 20, 1983), 66.

XV. War

Barasch, Marc Ian. "Aftermath—Nuclear Attack Would Alter Most Aspects of Current Civilizations," *Houston Chronicle* (November 1983).

Barasch, Marc Ian. "In Case of Nuclear Attack, Have All Your Numbers Ready and Get in Line," *Houston Chronicle* (October 20, 1983).

Culver, Robert. "Between War and Peace: Old Debate in a New Age," *Christianity Today* (October 24, 1980), 30–34.

Drescher, John. "Why Christians Shouldn't Carry Swords," *Christianity Today* (November 7, 1980), 15–23.

"Evangelical Christians Disagree on Nuclear Arms at Meeting," *Houston Chronicle* (May 30, 1983).

"Evangelicals Support N-arms Freeze—poll," *Houston Chronicle* (July 7, 1983).

"Faith and the Fate of the Earth," *Eternity* (October 1982), 21–29.

Frame, Randy. "Is the Road to Peace Paved with Might or with Meekness?" *Christianity Today* (July 15, 1983), 39–42.

Hook, Sidney. "We Must Not Give In," *Houston Chronicle* (May 16, 1983).

Kantzner, Kenneth S. "In Matters of War and Peace . . . ," *Christianity Today* (November 21, 1980), 14, 15.

Kantzner, Kenneth S. "What Shall We Do about the Nuclear Problem?" *Christianity Today* (January 21, 1983), 9–11.

Krauthammer, Charles. "Pacifism's Invisible Current," *Time* (May 30, 1983), 87, 88.

Lewis, Flora. "World Can't Shake Habit of War," *Houston Chronicle* (September 15, 1983).

Moyer, Robert L. "The Christian and War," *The Sword of the Lord* (July 1, 1983) 1, 10.

Pierard, Richard. "NAE's Social Awareness Grows," *Christianity Today* (April 9, 1982), 42.

"Return to God," *Time* (May 23, 1983), 57.

"Seek Nuclear Edge over Russia?" *U. S. News & World Report* (date unknown), 37, 38.

Thieme, R. B., Jr. *War—Moral or Immoral.* Houston: Berachak Tapes and Publications, n.d.

Tower, John. "In Defense of Defense," *Houston Chronicle* (February 14, 1983).

Wallace, James. "Nuclear Freeze Crusade," *U. S. News & World Report* (October 25, 1983), 18–21.

"War's Relentless Cost—It Doesn't End," *U. S. News & World Report* (October 25, 1982), 80, 81.

Watson, Russell. "Zia Bars the Door," *Newsweek* (October 13, 1980), 65.

Wilkerson, David. *The Cross and the Switchblade.* Pyramid Publications, 1971.

Woodward, Kenneth L. "Rendering unto Caesar," *Christian Beacon* (January 20, 1983).

Zalisk, Robert. "Nuclear Strategy—A Guide for the Beginner," NOVA. Boston: WGBH Transcripts.